"STAGE PLAY"
A Comedy Theatrical Stage Play

by

James Russell

Purchasing this script does not authorize performance rights. Please contact publisher before performing to negotiate terms & conditions. This script may or may not be available for production.

To locate publisher, in the event we move type: "James Russell Publishing" in any Internet search engine. Try also an updated edition of the Thomas Register at your library.

DEDICATION TO:
"It is a good thing to give thanks unto the Lord." Psalm 92.1

A THOUGHT TO PONDER:
There are over 800 promises in the Bible. Have you read them?

TABLE OF CONTENTS

TITLE PAGE

"Stage Play – A Comedy Theatrical Play"

© Pau2-217-929. October 28, 1997 by James Russell.
ISBN # 0-916367-34-7 (Print Version)
ISBN # 0-916367-47-9 (e-book Version)

James Russell Publishing
780 Diogenes Drive
Reno, NV 89512
Web: www.powernet.net/~scrnplay
E-mail: scrnplay@powernet.net
SAN # 295-852X

"Stage Play – A Comedy Theatrical Play"

Written by James Russell
First prepress Printed © April 1999.
First Printed edition © September 2001 0-916367-34-7.
E-book edition August © 2000 ISBN 0-916367-47-9.
Printed in the USA

THIS PLAY CAN BE PURCHASED FROM

-- Amazon.Com Books - www.amazon.com
-- Barnes & Noble - www.barnesandnoble.com or bookstore in your area.
-- Borders Books - www.borders.com or bookstore in your area.
-- Books A Million - www.booksamillion.com or bookstore in your area.
-- Chapters (Canada) - www.chapters.ca or bookstore in your area.
-- Lou's Books, 5647 Atlantic Ave, Long Beach, CA 90805 (213)423-1403.
-- Opamp Technical Books, 1033 N. Sycamore Ave, Los Angeles, CA 90038
(800)468-4322.
-- Varsity Books - see Internet or college bookstore.
-- Walden Books
-- Your local bookstore and e-book outlet kiosks.
-- We have a bookstore listing on our Web site.

Any bookstore can order this book. Just give them this number:
ISBN # 0-916367-25-8 and our SAN #295-852X.   To locate us in the event we move type: James
Russell Publishing in any Internet search engine.

ACT I

SCENE A

SETTING: TWO BEDROOMS. STAGE 2 CURTAINED.

AT RISE:

STAGE 1.

>   (SAMANTHA PETUNIA PANTHER (29) lies in
>   bed, snoring. Cigarette dangles from
>   lips. Hair and face a wreck. This gal
>   believes she is fat, but isn't.)

STAGE 3.

>   (MARY BEE CANARY (29)wakes up, dials
>   phone. Her hair's electrified. She's
>   a well-built, dim-witted, incompetent
>   woman.)
>
>   (Phone rings. Samantha fumbles to
>   answers it.)

                              MARY
              (all smiles, on phone, slurred speech)
      Rise and shine, Sam, you fat piece of trash.

>   (Mary applies makeup as she talks. She
>   too is in bed.)

                              SAMANTHA
      Uh? Oh? It's you, Mary. Why must you cast insults
      upon the waking hour? It sets up my day rotten.

>   (Samantha removes wine bottle and ash
>   tray from under covers, has a hangover,
>   twirls finger in ashes.)

                              MARY
      Because it's my way of being beautiful, honey, by
      making others feel ugly.
              (laughs, lights cigarette)

>   (Samantha wipes ashes on eyebrows,
>   grabs mirror, sees smearing.)

                              SAMANTHA
      You know how I feel about my face in the morning.

MARY

Then stop gawking at it. It's only a face. So what
if it looks like a dried up old fish--

        (Samantha slams mirror to floor.)

SAMANTHA

Stop it! I'm not going.

MARY

Why? Now what?

SAMANTHA

I look like a toad, feel like a bitch, and I can't
find my --

        (Samantha's hand searches under sheets.)

MARY

Your underwear is under the bed.

        (Samantha's hand locates underwear.
        Samantha grimaces, confused.)

SAMANTHA

What were you doing in my bed last night?

MARY

I had to tuck you in.

SAMANTHA

Nooo? I wasn't that drunk. Was I?

        (Samantha rubs head, painfully. Sips
        wine bottle, gags.)

SAMANTHA
    (continuing)
What the hell did you give me?

        (Mary laughs)

MARY

Just a little pick-me-up something.

        (Samantha swings legs from covers.
        Wears comic raccoon slippers.)

SAMANTHA

Gosh, why do we do these stupid things?

        (Samantha exits bed in her "Clucky
        Chicken" feed sack nightie, stumbles
        about drunk, stubs toe, falls down.)

MARY
Because we are girls, Sam. Girls. We were born to
be vulnerable.

                              (Samantha rises, rubs sore toe, OW!)

SAMANTHA
     (upset, still on phone)
I don't want to be vulnerable! I want to be in
control of my life.
     (fist pounds chest)
I want to be me, me, me!

MARY
Sassy little bitch you are today?

SAMANTHA
I'm sorry if I sound selfish, but my life revolves
around three people. Me, myself and I.

MARY
It shows.

SAMANTHA
And what is that supposed to mean?

MARY
Look in the mirror, babe.

                              (Samantha stands to wall mirror, gasps
                              at what she sees.)

MARY
     (continuing)
Within you, darling are three fat chicks just
screaming to get out of your bloated body.

                              (Samantha frowns, insulted.)

SAMANTHA
     (lying)
I'm not that fat. I can't help it I have big bones.

MARY
Huge vertebrae in your tush, honey?

                              (Samantha poses in mirror.)

SAMANTHA
Cartilage, darling. It's a temporary side effect of
colonic irrigation treatments. Nothing to sniff at.

MARY
Go ahead, take a good long look. Strain your eyes.

SAMANTHA
I don't want to look in the mirror.

                    (Samantha looks around, bewildered.
                    Gazes at her rear in mirror.)

              MARY

Bend over and touch your toes and look over your
shoulder. What do you see?

                    (Samantha bends, looks in mirror, gasps
                    in horror.)

              MARY
      (continuing)
That a girl. You'd make a fine Sumo wrestler, Sam.
You could make millions in Japan.

                    (Samantha rises, disgusted, paces,
                    lights cigarette.)

              SAMANTHA

Why must I be so fat? It's not fair to have such
huge body parts hanging on my skeleton like this.
If my fat could speak I'd be deaf by now.
      (yells)
I want to be thin!

                    (Samantha grabs chocolate bar from
                    drawer, slowly chews with self-
                    pity.)

              MARY

You're doing it again, Sam. Eating aren't you?

              SAMANTHA
      (child-like)
I can't help it. I always get hungry when I'm
depressed.

              MARY

You don't have to be.

                    (Samantha's foot slams floor.)

              SAMANTHA
      (shouts)
I want to be!

              MARY

I'll be there in ten.

                    (They hang up. Samantha paces,
                    mumbles, stuffs chocolate in her mouth.)

                    (Mary exits bed with full attire of
                    sexy clothing. Swigs gin bottle on
                    dresser. Checks wall calendar, stuffs
                    hair under a hat, grabs pocketbook and
                    exits.)

                           SAMANTHA
         (to herself, posing to mirror)
I'm not that bad looking. There are curves to be
seen, if I bend the right way.
         (snaps)
So what if my buns have risen?
         (calm)
There's more to love.
         (explodes)
I hate being fat!

                              (Samantha grabs wine bottle, guzzles,
                              takes a huge bite of chocolate, chokes
                              on it.)

                              (She taps bird cage. A mechanical
                              parrot cat-call whistles at her.)

                           PARROT
Awk! You look fine, baby.

                           SAMANTHA
That's better.

                              (Nose to cage, kissing.)

                           SAMANTHA
         (continuing)
Talk to me, honey.

                           PARROT
Lovely girl. Can I hug you to sleep tonight? Awk!

                              (Samantha tosses candy wrapper in the
                              overflowing trash can. She tries to
                              empty trash, spills contents.)

                           SAMANTHA
I need a man to take out this trash.
         (yells)
I don't know how to do it!

                              (Knock on door. Samantha hides candy
                              in drawer. Mary enters, heads straight
                              to drawer, removes packages of candy.)

                           MARY
I knew it.

                           SAMANTHA
         (talks with mouth full)
What do you know? Those candies could have been
there for six-months.

                           PARROT
Liar! Liar! Awk!

                       SAMANTHA
    (to Parrot, screams)
Shut-up!

                              (Samantha tosses blanket over cage.)

                       SAMANTHA
    (continuing)
Eating lifts my spirit... and leaves this carcass
behind. The devil makes me do it!

                              (Mary grabs Samantha's jaws, sees
                              chocolate in mouth.)

                       MARY
Spit it out! Spit it out!

                              (Samantha wags head.)

                       MARY
    (continuing)
Don't you dare swallow it!

                              (Mary squeezes Samantha's throat.
                              Samantha swallows, smiles. Mary lets
                              go, paces.)

                       MARY
    (continuing)
It's no use. I've tried everything doctor
Spittlebug advised, but nooo, you won't obey.

                       SAMANTHA
I enjoy being rebellious. I'll do what I want in
this life.
    (pounds finger to chest)
For me, me, me!

                       MARY
And what about me? I have to be seen with a --

                       SAMANTHA
What?

                       MARY
Nothing.

                       SAMANTHA
You were going to say it, weren't you?
    (snaps)
Then say it!

                       MARY
Leave it alone.

                              (Samantha paces. Mary bites lip.)

                              SAMANTHA
I won't. That was a low blow, Mary. All these
years we've been friends--

                              MARY
I didn't say anything. So stuff that up your poop-
chute and sit on it.

                              SAMANTHA
I thought we agreed we would never speak on that
subject again?

                         (Mary looks to floor.)

                              MARY
I'm sorry, Sam.
     (looks up)
But, I didn't say it.

                              (Samantha prances with gloating
                              satisfaction.)

                              MARY
     (continuing)
However... it's time you find a man and get married.

                              (Samantha covers ears. Mary presses
                              on, face-to-face.)

                              MARY
     (continuing)
Well it's true! You can't hide from the truth.

                              (Samantha dodges to no use.)

                              SAMANTHA
I don't want to hear it. Stop it! Stop!

                              (Mary grabs Samantha's arms, pulls them
                              down from ears.)

                              MARY
Happy birthday, Sam.

                              (Samantha's face distorts with horror.
                              Hands bat the air shooing Mary away.)

                              SAMANTHA
So it's true.

                              (Samantha's drained of energy, falls to
                              bed, weeps.)

                              MARY
It was destined to happen. You knew that. It's no
big deal.

> SAMANTHA
> (tearfully)
> I hate birthdays.   They make me depressed.

>> (Mary sighs, approaches carefully)

> MARY
> It's time.

>> (Samantha gasps, hand to mouth.   Leaps
>> from bed, scuttles to mirror.)

> SAMANTHA
> Nooo! It can't be? The end of my world?
>   (grief)
> Oh death, comes upon me like a thief in the night.

>> (Samantha's shoulders droop with
>> resignation.   Mary touches shoulder.)

> SAMANTHA
> (continuing)
> Don't touch me!

>> (Samantha distances herself.)

> MARY
> It's only a birthday.

>> (Samantha purses lips.)

> SAMANTHA
> (rising anger)
> Oh, easy for you to say. It my birthday, not yours.
> I'm the one who has to face reality, not you. I
> have to face the demise of my womanhood. I'm the
> one that's doomed to live with scornful eyes
> trailing my every movements.
>   (Samantha mimics people pointing)
> "Look at her." "What's wrong with that girl?" Why
> can't she find a life?"

>> (Samantha vibrates, anxiety attack.
>> Mary removes pill from pocket, jams
>> into Samantha's mouth, slaps cheeks.)

> MARY
> Come, now, sweetheart. It'll help you calm down.

> SAMANTHA
> What the hell was it?

> MARY
> I don't know? Some guys gave 'em to me last night.

>> (Samantha panics, faces audience.)

                        SAMANTHA
Oh, my gosh! It could kill me!

                        (Mary frowns, shrugs shoulders.)

                        SAMANTHA
     (continuing; perplexed)
What guys? Here? In my room? Am I with child?

                        (Samantha searches for wet sheets.)

                        MARY
No such luck, Sam. They loaded us up and didn't
fire the gun. Bastards!

                        (Samantha's relieved.)

                        SAMANTHA
Dry sheets.

                        (Samantha feels wetness, eyes expand.)

                        MARY
Wine, darling. It's only wine you spilled.

                        SAMANTHA
Thank bloody gawd. The thought of being hit and run
like that... if a man is to sleep with a woman he
should at least stick around 'till the sun rises.

                        MARY
Only a hus-

                        (Samantha cover ears.)

                        SAMANTHA
Do not say that word in this house!

                        (Mary yanks Samantha's hands down.)

                        MARY
     (yells)
You listen to me! It's your birthday. It happens
to everyone. You should at least be grateful for it.

                        SAMANTHA
     (screams)
This is not the typical birthday. It's the dreaded
one, the one that means death. Look at me. My face
is wrinkling as I speak.

                        MARY
For heaven's sake, Sam. You're only thir-

                        (Samantha cover ears tightly.)

                        MARY
        (continuing; shouts)
You're thirty! You hear me? Thirty! Thirty!

                        SAMANTHA
        (disconsolate)
Noooo! Go away. I'm too old to have a friend. I
can hear the shovels trenching the earth and the
dirt sprinkling upon my casket.

                              (Mary forces wine down Samantha's
                              throat.)

                        MARY
Now, now. It's okay. That a girl, let it all hang
out. Get it off your chest.

                              (Samantha breaks away, looks hard,
                              wipes wine from her mouth.)

                        SAMANTHA
Oh? So you're in on it too?

                        MARY
In on what?

                        SAMANTHA
The world conspiracy?

                              (Mary sighs. Mimics gun to head.)

                        MARY
Where's your Prozac?

                        SAMANTHA
You know what I'm talking about.

                        MARY
It's not a conspiracy, Sam. It's life. It's the
way the world turns. It's just your time--

                        SAMANTHA
Time? Time?

                              (Samantha looks to clock, wheezes.)

                        SAMANTHA
        (continuing)
Oh ma-gosh! We'll be late for the rehearsal.

                        MARY
What rehearsal?

                              (Samantha checks wall calendar, finger
                              slams to a date.)

                              SAMANTHA
This one.

                                        (Note: Alter date to reflect
                                        performance date in next dialog.)

                              MARY
It's not 1999, Sam. It's 1998. You have the wrong
page.

                              SAMANTHA
I do?

                                        (Samantha, flips calendar pages.
                                        Samantha gulps, covers her mouth. Mary
                                        and Samantha lock eyes.)

                              SAMANTHA
        (continuing)
Happy birthday, Mary.

                                        (Mary stands in shock.)

                              MARY
Noooo!

                                        (Samantha's hands to hips.)

                              SAMANTHA
        (no mercy)
So what's the big deal? So what it's your birthday
and your thirty--

                                        (Mary cover her ears.)

                              SAMANTHA
        (continuing)
You need a damn husband!

                                        (Samantha grabs Mary's arms, pulls
                                        hands from ears.)

                              MARY
It can't be?

                              SAMANTHA
It is. Time never lies. Look in the mirror.

                                        (Samantha pushes Mary to mirror.)

                              SAMANTHA
        (continuing)
Your hips are widening, gravity's tugging on your
boobs soon to be swinging aimlessly by your navel.
Bags are forming under your eyes. You need a surgeon.

                                        (Samantha pokes finger under Mary's
                                        chin.)

                              SAMANTHA
        (continuing)
I see a baby double-chin being conceived in the womb
of antiquity. Look at you!

You better get a husband now before it's too late.
You've run out of time, babe. You're old!

                              (Mary paces. Hands squeeze head.)

                              MARY
How could you be so cruel? You tricked me.

                              SAMANTHA
You would have done it to me.

                              MARY
        (eyes searching)
I would not.

                              SAMANTHA
Who cares? We're both in deep sheep's poop up to
our mascara. We got to do what we got to do.

                              MARY
Oh, no. That we can't do.

                              SAMANTHA
So, you want to end up an old spinster? A mocking
bird with no nest to call home?
        (mimics people pointing)
"Oh, look at Mary. Her womb is empty and has no man
to fill it." "Such a pitiful woman to behold."

                              MARY
People won't say those things. Oh, damn. What are
we going to do? All this fun in life up in smoke.

                              SAMANTHA
It's time to put our emergency plan into action.

                              MARY
Sam! That was a joke. Stupid girl-talk. We were
drunk, stoned, out of it. You're not serious.

                              (Samantha's serious.)

                              MARY
        (continuing)
I don't know if we should even consider such a
notion. It's unnatural.

                              SAMANTHA
Age is unnatural. Men are natural fools. We just
set'em up and our problems are over.

                              (Mary thinks hard. Samantha puts on
                              clothes, fixes her hair.)

                         MARY
What if people find out?

                         SAMANTHA
Tsk. How will they?

                         MARY
If my mother did, I'd be banished from the nest. I
mean it. She's too Christian for such thinking.

                         SAMANTHA
Darling. Life is not fair. It's only just for
those who take things.
     (slyly)
All we're gonna do is take a couple husbands.

                              (Mary's back stiffens.)

                         MARY
I won't fiddle with married instruments.

                         SAMANTHA
I said take husbands, not steal them. Do you
understand the meaning of this?

                              (Mary's confused, brows sink.)

                         MARY
Oh, now I know. Yes! Yes! Oh, wow. To think we
are actually going to pull this off. But wait a
minute. Who? Who are we going to snag?

                         SAMANTHA
Remember we talked about --

                         MARY
Yes. But--

                              (Samantha covers Mary's mouth with
                              hand.)

                         . SAMANTHA
Shush-up! This place could be bugged.

                         MARY
Bugged? Why? By who?

                         SAMANTHA
By two lonely bastards who may be pursuing the same
fantasy. If any traps are to be set, I'll be the
one to set them, not the other way around.

                         MARY
Right! I agree.

                              SAMANTHA
It's high time you see the light.   You only have
three days.

                              MARY
          (gasps)
Three days?

                              (Mary races to calendar, crumples it to
                              floor, stomps on it.)

CURTAIN FALLS - REMOVE BEDS FROM STAGE.

(END OF SCENE A)

                        SCENE B

STAGE 2.

SETTING: A NIGHT CLUB.   STAGE 1 & 3 INTEGRAL TO STAGE 2.

AT RISE:

                              (Rehearsals taking place. DISCJOCKEY
                              plays music in b.g. ACTORS and
                              ACTRESSES dash about on stage.
                              SAMANTHA and MARY arrive, acting as
                              elegant ladies.)

                              (Two macho dudes, DELBERT PIMPLEFACE
                              (35) and SIMON CROTCHITCH (33) notice,
                              elbow each other. They approach.
                              Delbert wears red satin shirt. Macho
                              dudes, gold chains, etc.)

                              DELBERT
Hi, babes.

                              SIMON
Whoa, cuties.   Shake those buns for me.

                              (Samantha and Mary smirk, ignore them,
                              cross to bar.)

                              SAMANTHA
Mary, I think we found our stupid little chickens.

                              MARY
What about the other guys?

                              SAMANTHA
Forget them.   It's their loss not ours.

                              (Mary and Samantha examine Delbert and
                              Simon.)

                        MARY
Damn, they're good looking too! I want the guy in
the red shirt.

                        SAMANTHA
I wanted him!

                             (Samantha and Mary peek at the two men.
                              Simon picks his nose.)

                        SAMANTHA
     (continuing)
On second thought--

                        MARY
I'm so damn desperate I'd take either one. I just
need a man. Any man!

                        SAMANTHA
Husband.

                        MARY
Yeah, whatever. All I've ever wanted was to love
and be loved. I've got to get married, Sam. I only
have three days. This is an emergency.

                        SAMANTHA
Can't count today, darling. This day is half gone
already. You only have two days left.

                        MARY
Oh, my gosh. I'm scared, Sam. Time's running out.

                             (Producer ALEX GETHIGH (40) arrives.)

                        ALEX
Samantha Petunia Panther? Mary Bee Canary? I'm
Alex Gethigh, producer.

                             (Samantha and Mary nod, shake hands.
                              Delbert and Simon watch.)

                        ALEX
     (continuing)
Your agent tells me you're both super-duper
actresses.

                        MARY
Super-duper in more ways than one, babe.

                             (Samantha elbows Mary.)

                        MARY
     (continuing)
Ow!

                        SAMANTHA
     (lip-speaks)
He's too old.

(Mary rubs ribs. Samantha smiles,
elegantly. Delbert and Simon smile.)

                    SAMANTHA
     (continuing)
I'd like to see the contract. I've been around this
block too many times to not ask.

                    ALEX
No problem.

                         (Alex removes contract from briefcase.
                         Samantha examines it.)

                    ALEX
     (continuing)
It's legit.

                    SAMANTHA
Appears in order.

                         (Samantha returns contract.)

                    SAMANTHA
     (continuing)
Mail it to my agent.

                         (Alex smiles.)

                    ALEX
     (to everyone on stage)
Step off please. Shut off the music, please.

                         (Music off. Alex slips Samantha and
                         Mary scripts, gently fingers Samantha's
                         rear, caresses Mary's thigh.)

                    ALEX
     (continuing; to Samantha)
Stand over here, dear.
     (to Mary)
We'll block you right here. Good.

                         (Alex remains on stage. Samantha and
                         Mary appear bewildered.)

                    MARY
     (reading line)
Oh, look, Petunia. The buzzards are circling upon
the sun. Do you think they will see us?

                         (Both wipe foreheads, look dehydrated.
                         Mary sips whisky from bottle, coughs,
                         gags, angrily spits it to floor.)

                    MARY
     (continuing; to Alex)
Hey? This is real whisky?

                         (Delbert and Simon laugh.)

                              ALEX
We do it right in this theater. We don't fake
nothing. Notice how the scene took, huh? Even the
cough and gagging was true to life.

                            SAMANTHA
     (reading line)
We'll never make it out of here alive. I told you
we shouldn't have robbed that bank.

                              MARY
     (reading line)
To hell with the bank. I'm more concerned with them
damned buzzards. The thought of being eaten alive,
beaks tearing into my flesh like scissors. I need
a drink!

                                   (Samantha guzzles champagne bottle.
                                   They fight for it, guzzle it down dry.
                                   They are drunk.)

                              MARY
     (continuing)
I, uh, stish it, I mean stuff it, tootsie it's my--

                            SAMANTHA
Ga to, ah, oh damn my, my lips just--

                                   (Alex moves in, attempts to remove
                                   their clothes. Samantha and Mary
                                   scream.)

                              MARY
What is happening here? Get your grimy hands off me.

                            SAMANTHA
That's not in the script. Who are you?

                              ALEX
Relax, babes. We're all here for a little clean fun.

                                   (Mary bites Alex's hand like a lizard.
                                   Samantha screams, kicks Alex in groin.)

                              ALEX
     (continuing)
Ow!

                                   (Mary and Samantha stagger to bar
                                   vibrating in rage.)

                              ALEX
     (continuing)
Ha! Can't take a joke?
                              SIMON
Man, that wasn't too cool.

DELBERT
We're not into this trash.

ALEX
So what? It's show business. I'm one of the
sleezeballs you read about in the tabloids.

        (Delbert and Simon grab Alex, toss him
        out the door. They high-five.)

        (Delbert and Simon approach Samantha
        and Mary.)

DELBERT
I beg your pardon, ladies.

        (Samantha and Mary stare, meanly.
        Still vibrating.)

DELBERT
   (continuing; to Bartender.)
Sweet wine for the ladies, please.

SAMANTHA	MARY
We don't drink. We're not that kind of women.	We don't drink. We're not that kind of women.

        (Women at bar angrily stare.)

DELBERT
One drink won't kill ya?

SIMON
   (to Mary)
I wasn't involved with that scene.

        (Mary melts. Samantha stomps her foot
        OW! Bartender delivers wine. They
        move to F.)

DELBERT
Let's dance, please?

        (Samantha thinks, then nods. Mary does
        the same. They place drinks on coffee
        table.)

        (Discjockey spins song, "Newborn
        Friends" by Seal. They dance to the
        fast beat.)

        (Mary keeps bumping chest-on into Simon
        on purpose.)

SIMON
I'm sorry.

                                    MARY
Don't be.

                              (Delbert and Simon both snap fingers
                              behind their backs. Discjockey
                              switches to slow romantic song, "Don't
                              Cry" by Seal.)

                              (Mary leaps on Simon. Samantha stands
                              shy and sad. Delbert gently takes her
                              in arms.)

                              (Mary steps on Simon's toes, then bends
                              Simon over for a big long kiss. He
                              fights to breath.)

                              (When lyrics hit, "Don't cry..."
                              Samantha cries. Delbert wipes her
                              eyes. A touching scene. They hug
                              closely to the music, swaying.)

                              (After a few moments, Bartender walks
                              by, shakes his head. Pulls the plug.
                              Music stops.)

                              DELBERT
Hey? What gives?

                              BARTENDER
I'm sorry, but this song makes me cry.

                              (Samantha and Mary cry, dash to coffee
                              table, take good swig of wine. Delbert
                              and Simon follow, lift drinks.)

                              DELBERT
May we toast?

                              SAMANTHA
Two fine gentlemen. Knight's in shining armor
rescue the fair maidens from the evil producer.

                              SIMON
Yeah, that's a good one.

                              (They cling glasses, sip wine.)

                              (Samantha and Mary toss wine into
                              Delbert and Simon's face.)

            SAMANTHA   MARY
        It's not, Korbel!   It's not, Korbel!

                              (Samantha and Mary storm out R.)
                              SIMON
What was that all about?

DELBERT
(to Bartender)
I ought to bust your lip. The wine's not Korbel.

BARTENDER
That does it. Look, this is a bar room, not a
theater. I agreed you guys could rehearse here, but
no more. It's over.

DELBERT
Whoa, sergeant. We're just actors. We didn't know
anything about that Alex.

SIMON
That's right. We're innocent.

BARTENDER
You single men are all alike. Lies, lies, lies.
Will do anything to get into a woman's bed then cry
like babies when it's time to propose.

DELBERT   SIMON
I can't argue with that.   I can't argue with that.

(Samantha and Mary enter with police.)

SAMANTHA
(to Delbert and Simon)
Where is that sonofabitch?

DELBERT
We tossed the bum out.

MARY
Sure you did. You were in on it too.
(to police)
Arrest those sinful men.

(Police slap on cuffs.)

DELBERT
Look man, ya got it all wrong.

DELBERT
(continuing; to Samantha)
We didn't do nothing to you. Alex is the s.o.b.

SAMANTHA
S.O.B? Meaning, "Sorry old bugger?"

MARY
Teach you for taking advantage of a lady.

SIMON
(sniveling)
I'm innocent.

                              SAMANTHA
We are superior to you men.

                                   (Police exit with Delbert and Simon
                                   arguing loudly as they go.)

                              SAMANTHA
          (continuing)
This business sucks!

                                MARY
All I want is a husband.
          (scolding)
It was your selfish desire to become an actress made
you immoral.

                              SAMANTHA
What? What about you, Saint Mary?

                                MARY
I simply followed you into this hellish life.

                                   (Stagehands circle them.)

                          FIRST STAGE HAND
          (to Mary)
I'm not married. Would you consider me?

                          SECOND STAGE HAND
          (to Samantha)
I may only have a face a mother could love, but
marrying me would, ya'know, make you a mother and
then you could find it in your heart to love me.

               SAMANTHA   MARY
              No way!   No way!

                                   (Everyone exits.)

                              SAMANTHA
Bloody mess you got us into!

                                MARY
Me?

                              SAMANTHA
Yes, you. It's your birthday! You're the one who
needs a damn husband, not me.

                                MARY
Until next month.

                                   (Samantha's shocked.)

                                MARY
          (continuing)
It's no use arguing, darling. We're both in the
same boat and it's sinking fast.

                  (Mary grabs her throat, mimics
                  drowning. They laugh. PEOPLE enter,
                  music plays.)

               SAMANTHA

What's this?

               MARY

It's a night club. We were setup by a conman, Sam.
Typical glamour scam. Just like when we won that
cruiseship vacation to Rhode Island, remember? When
the ship sailed and it wasn't supposed to?

               SAMANTHA

Shush! Someone who was on that boat could be here
and destroy our reputations. I need a drink.

                  (Samantha leaves, Mary grabs Samantha's
                  collar, yanked to a stop.)

               MARY

You're already half-cocked.

               SAMANTHA

Shhhh! Don't say that word. You know it makes me
anxious. Do you have anymore of them pills?

                  (Mary searches pockets, hash pipe,
                  cigarette papers, but no pills.)

               MARY

Don't worry. I can get more.

                  (Samantha flails hands, stamps feet.)

               SAMANTHA

   (shouts)
I want them now!

                  (Music stops, everyone stares.
                  Samantha smiles. Music resumes.
                  People dance.)

               MARY

Stop making a scene.

               SAMANTHA

Is that what you want? Just stand here and let
every man just pass you by unnoticed?
   (yells)
I'm trying to help you gain a little publicity.

                  (People's heads turn.)

               MARY

There is no reason to cause embarrassment.

                          SAMANTHA

Embarrassment?
     (laughs)
What do I do to cause you embarrassment, hmmm? Tell
me. What do I do to make you ashamed of me?

                          MARY

When you scratch your tush in public.

                              (Samantha gasps with shock, finger
                              scratches her butt.)

                          MARY
     (continuing)
See? You're doing it.
                               (Samantha catches herself. Jerks hand
                              away, looks around, embarrassed.)

                          SAMANTHA

I can't help it. It's just a little nervous twitch
I have. Gosh, this is embarrassing.
     (shouts)
I was born this way!

                              (People stare and smirk. Samantha and
                              Mary sit at bar.)

                          SAMANTHA
     (continuing; to Bartender.)
Wine, please. Good wine.

                              (Bartender slams two bottles to
                              bar.)

                              (Mary and Samantha try to open foil on
                              bottle, break nails OW!)

                          SAMANTHA
     (continuing; to Bartender)
Look what you did.

                          MARY

Do you have any idea how serious these injuries are?

                              (Samantha lifts bottle, looks at label.)

                          SAMANTHA

Infidel! We want Zinfandel.

                              (Bartender exchanges bottles.)

                          SAMANTHA
     (continuing; to Bartender.)
You can dump the attitude. This isn't Ceasar's
Palace.

MARY
        (to Bartender)
I want Red Wolf beer.

BARTENDER
We got, Red Dog. Take it or leave it.

SAMANTHA
Stop arguing with her.

MARY
I don't like Red Dog.

                        (Man with red hair at bar frowns.)

BARTENDER
Look ladies --

SAMANTHA
How about, King Cobra beer?

MARY
I'd settle for, Wicked Pete.

                        (Awful dressed man wearing white cowboy
                        boots at bar, turns, smiles. Bartender
                        points to the man.)

BARTENDER
That's wicked Pete.

                        (Bartender delivers King Cobra beer.
                        Samantha and Mary guzzle it. Pete
                        approaches.)

                        (Samantha and Mary shoo him away making
                        strange sounds. They sit on couch.)

SAMANTHA
        (to Bartender, demanding.)
Tequila. We want Tequila.

MARY
What's wrong with that man?

BARTENDER
Hold your temper, I'm busy.

SAMANTHA
I'm thirsty, hurry up. They can wait.

                        (People's heads turn, sneer. Samantha
                        and Mary sneer back.)

                        (Bartender delivers two bottles of
                        Tequila.)

                          MARY
Where's the worm?
     (yells)
I want the worm.

                                   (Men at bar look, smile.)

                          SAMANTHA
     (to men)
Filthy pigs. Mind your own business.

                              (Samantha and Mary elegantly dip
                              pretzels into beer then guzzle Tequila
                              straight from bottle.)

                          MARY
Bartender! Bartender! Get me some Rattlesnake
whiskey.

                          SAMANTHA
And don't take all day!

                              (Bartender stares angrily. Waitress
                              arrives, pats him on shoulder.)

                          MARY
Incompetence. I can't stand incompetence.

                              (Mary fumbles with makeup mirror.
                              Samantha grabs and opens it for her.)

                              (Samantha removes her mirror. They
                              both apply makeup.)

                              (Mary's hands shake, wipes lipstick
                              across her cheek. Samantha dips napkin
                              in beer, wipes Mary's cheek.)

                          MARY
     (continuing)
Bloody incompetency drives me insane.

                          SAMANTHA
I know. Men, they are such idiots.
     (yells)
Half of the men in here need makeup. If they wised
up they wouldn't be here in this bar alone.

                              (Men at bar turn and stare. Samantha
                              and Mary wave finger in circle. Men
                              turn around.)

                          SAMANTHA
     (continuing)
See how easy it is to control them?

                              (Samantha stuffs ashtray down blouse.)

MARY

What are you doing? You said you broke that habit,
Sam. It's not a man's hand. Stop it.

SAMANTHA
   (embarrassed)
Tsk. I don't do that anymore. I just want the
ashtray.

                     (Mary removes stick deodorant, applies
                     it under arms. Samantha pulls out a
                     Mademoiselle magazine and reads.)

                     (Mary pulls out can of dog food, eats
                     it.)

SAMANTHA
   (continuing)
Gawd! Mary!

MARY

What?

SAMANTHA

That's dog food.

                     (Mary looks at label, befuddled.)

MARY

I grabbed it off the shelf in the supermarket. I
thought it was tuna. What the hell are they selling
dog food in a human supermarket for?
   (beat, screams)
I'll sue!
                     (Men at bar scatter. Bartender stops
                     them at exit.)

SAMANTHA
How many years have you been eating this?

                     (Mary stares, thinking in a daze.)

SAMANTHA
   (continuing)
Darling, it's okay. I haven't heard you bark yet.
What do they put in that anyway?

                     (Samantha grabs can, gasps.)

MARY
What? What?

                     (Samantha tosses can, plows onto bar
                     PING!)

SAMANTHA
You don't want to know.

                                    (Wicked Pete fingers the can, eats
                                    contents. Smiles at Mary.)

                        MARY
He's looking at me again, Sam. Maybe I can change
him.

                        SAMANTHA
Darling, the only thing you'll be changing on him is
his underwear and soiled sheets. He's a bloody
drunken beast of a man. You can do better.

                        MARY
I hope so. Time is running out, Sam. I've got to
have a man. I need a man. I'm afraid, Sam. What
if I never get married?

                                    (Mary cries. Sam comforts her. Places
                                    cigarette in her lips, makes her sip
                                    Tequila.)

                        SAMANTHA
Feel better now?

                                    (Mary nods, wipes mouth with arm.)

                        SAMANTHA
        (continuing)
We could rent a husband.

                        MARY
Rent a husband? How?

                        SAMANTHA
Escort service.

                        MARY
It's not the same. I mean, I want someone I can
control. Someone I can manipulate and punish when
I'm feeling blue. You know?

                        SAMANTHA
Yeah, I know what you mean. It's just not the same
as having a real clown.

                        MARY
Bloody right. I want a real husband.

                        SAMANTHA
        (yells)
Yeah, and if he tries to rebel and walk out take
half of everything he's got.

                                    (Men at bar rise to leave. Bartender
                                    stops them.)

MARY

Damn right. I want the commitment. His grave stone
should say, "I said I do, and I done do regret it."
That's a relationship.

SAMANTHA

Precisely, 'till death do us part.

MARY

Him first.

SAMANTHA

Certainly. Who would possibly conceive of dying and
not being able to live the dream without all that
insurance money?

SAMANTHA	MARY
Nobody!	Nobody!

SAMANTHA

That's why women live longer.

MARY

It's our reward for cleaning up after his mess for
all those bloody years.

SAMANTHA

That's right. God made sure we would get our just
rewards. Inherently built it in us to live longer
than men.

MARY

Thank God for small miracles. Even if he is a man.

>   (Samantha looks to heaven, thinks,
>   looks around the ceiling. Points to
>   herself.)

SAMANTHA

    (to God)
Me? I didn't say that.
    (points to Mary)
She did!

>   (Mary pulls out a round granola bar,
>   bites into it. Samantha frowns.)

SAMANTHA

    (continuing)
Darling, that's bird seed cake.

>   (Mary spits seeds out.)

>   (Samantha grabs Mary's pocketbook,
>   pulls out can of insecticide.)

                        SAMANTHA
     (continuing)
Insecticide?

                        MARY
I thought it was feminine spray.

                        SAMANTHA
Better let me do the shopping, darling.

                        MARY
I can do it myself.

                              (Samantha stares, raises eyebrow. Mary
                              snatches insecticide.)

                        MARY
     (continuing)
Well, it stopped the itching.

                              (Samantha recoils in shock.)

                        SAMANTHA
Give that to me.

                              (They Tug-O-War.)

                        MARY
It's mine. Get your own.

                              (Can sprays. Bartender throws down
                              towel.)

                        BARTENDER
You no good little squirts. Get out of my bar.

                        WICKED PETE
Oh, no you don't.

                              (Pete and Bartender fight. Crowd
                              breaks them up. Crowd forces Bartender
                              to leave.)

                        BARTENDER
This is my joint. Get your hands off me. I own
this place.

                        PATRON
Take the day off.

                              (Bartender exits R.)

                              (Mary looks, recoils. Sees Delbert and
                              Simon enter, cross to bar.)
                        MARY
Uh, oh. Trouble.

> (Samantha and Mary jerk to feet.
> Samantha's ashtray slips from blouse,
> slams to Mary's toe OW! Sam covers
> Mary's mouth.)

> (They duck low, hide behind couch,
> peeking.)

                    DELBERT
Them dumb bitches.

                    SIMON
Yeah, I'd like to snap their necks like a chicken
bone.

> (Simon snaps pencil in two.)

> (Samantha and Mary's heads poke up,
> listening, hands to throat.)

> (Bartender enters, crosses to bar.)

                    DELBERT
Did you see the brains on that, Samantha?   Man,
they are perfectly round like basketballs.

> (Samantha frowns, peeks at her breasts.)

                    SIMON
Didn't notice, but I saw hamstrings that would fit
a bull.

> (Samantha stares meanly.)

                    DELBERT
What about that Hornpout she's with, Mary?

> (Samantha and Mary shocked. Mary lips
> the word,"Hornpout?" Mary rises in
> anger, Samantha yanks her back down.)

                    SIMON
Ah, forget 'em. Those girls are not ladies, they're
goonie-bird actresses and we all know how impure
they really are. So fine on the outside, yet deep
down inside they have filthy minds. I heard Joan
Rivers joke about it. She reveals truth, I can tell
you that!

> (Delbert nods. Samantha and Mary still
> peek, duck as Delbert glances.)

                    DELBERT
C'mon, Simon. Let's go pick up some real women.
> (Delbert and Simon exit. Samantha and
> Mary push through a couple holding
> hands as they move to F.)

                              MARY
Where did that bastard run?

                            SAMANTHA
        (yells)
Give me a gun!

                                        (People freeze, stare, resume dancing
                                        to soft music.)

                              MARY
Ah, to Hades with 'em. So what if they have the
finest muscular butt's I've seen in twenty-nine
years.

                            SAMANTHA
Thirty. You're thirty, in two days.

                                        (Mary storms to bar, grabs a man's
                                        drink, guzzles it. Takes another,
                                        repeats all the way down the bar.)

                                        (Bartender grabs Mary, picks her up,
                                        carries her to door. Samantha jumps on
                                        his back, biting, scratching. They
                                        tumble to floor.)

                            BARTENDER
Help! I'm being attacked by wild felines!

                                        (Nobody budges, nobody cares.)

                            SAMANTHA
        (to Bartender)
Leave her alone. She has rights!

                              MARY
        (screams)
I'm telling your wife!

                                        (Music stops. Everyone stares.
                                        Bartender lets go. They rise.)

                            SAMANTHA
That's right. You picked her up. We seen you do it!

                            SAMANTHA
        (continuing; yells)
Apologize to her!

                                        (Mary looking mean as a cat.)

                            BARTENDER
Don't pester the customers.
                                        (Bartender resumes his duties.)

MARY
The nerve of that foul-mouthed sonofabitch no good--

(Music resumes.)

SAMANTHA
Bastard! Let's sail to the ladies room. Conference
time.

(They exit to ladies room. Delbert and
Simon enter. Look around for Samantha
and Mary. Slow music plays.)

DELBERT
Damn, they're gone.

(Delbert and Simon ask two GIRLS to
dance. They smirk.)

DELBERT
(continuing)
What's the matter? Afraid you won't fit in my arms?

(Delbert takes her hand, they dance
slow. He tries to hug her tight, she
pushes back, smiles.)

(Simon snaps fingers, dances with other
girl.)

(Samantha and Mary exit, freeze seeing
them on dance floor.)

MARY
Look! The s.o.b's returned like homesick dogs.

SAMANTHA
What do those women have that I don't?

MARY
Big tits and slim hips.

SAMANTHA
There is way much more to a woman than body parts.

MARY
Beauty may be only skin deep, but that's what men
want.

(They stare with jealously. Samantha
begins to vibrate in anger, dashes
through dance floor, breaks up Delbert.)

SAMANTHA
(yells to girl)
He's mine!

(Girl wags her head, slaps Delbert,
storms away. Mary races to Simon,
breaks them apart. Second girl slaps
Simon, dashes away, returns, slaps him
again.)

SIMON

Ow!

DELBERT

What's going on here?

SAMANTHA
(to Delbert)
And just who do you think you are dancing with that
woman?

MARY
(yells)
They have V.D.!

(Everyone stops, stares, music stops.
Two girls totally embarrassed and
enraged approach.)

FIRST GIRL
(to Mary)
How dare you ridicule me in public?

SAMANTHA
(eyes searching)
They have V.D.!
(Samantha points to Delbert and Simon.)

DELBERT

Now wait a minute here--

MARY
(screams)
Shut up when she's speaking to you!

(Bartender storms over.)

BARTENDER

What's the meaning of this?

(Samantha and Mary try to walk away.
Bartender yanks them back by collars.)

SIMON

That's no way to treat a lady.

DELBERT

Take your hands off them fine broads.

SAMANTHA	MARY
Broads?	Broads?

                              (Samantha and Mary slap Delbert, and
                              Simon, OUCH! They storm out.
                              Bartender waves for music to begin.
                              People return to business, dance, etc.)

                    BARTENDER
Nothing but trouble them gals. If I were you I'd
disassociate yourselves from them dipwits... if you
can.

                    DELBERT
     (laughs)
What do you mean if you can?

                              (Delbert shows muscle in arm.
                              Bartender laughs. Delbert frowns.)

                    BARTENDER
All the muscle and atomic bombs in the world
couldn't stop a determined woman. They got the hots
for you boys.
     (laughs)
I hear wedding bells over the horizon.

                              (Bartender places hand to ear.)

                    BARTENDER
     (continuing; sings)
Wedding bells. Ding-a-ling--

                              (Simon knocks his hand down.)

                    SIMON
Women! Poohey on 'em. What could they do to make
me jump?

                              (Samantha and Mary enter, very upset,
                              screaming, pointing finger's at them.
                              Simon jumps.)

                    MARY
Freeze! Don't anybody touch them men!

                              (Music stops, everyone stares.)

                    SAMANTHA
     (to Delbert)
Get over here! I'm not finished with you, boy.

                              (Delbert and Simon run, exit.
                              Bartender's hands in air, backs away.)

                    SAMANTHA
     (continuing; to Mary)
See? I told you it would work.

MARY

Yeah, chased them right out of here too. Now what
do we do? I need a husband! And so do you!

SAMANTHA

Shhhh! People can hear you.
     (to people staring)
Go on, go on about your business.

                         (Samantha waves her hands about,
                         prances around. People return to
                         business, fast music plays.)

MARY

I'm scared, Sam. What if it doesn't work? What if
they don't come back? What if I become a day older
with no husband? What if--

SAMANTHA

Shut up!

                         (Samantha paces, thinks.)

SAMANTHA

     (continuing)
They'll come back.

                         (They stand looking at entry. Samantha
                         and Mary look stood-up, angry. Two MEN
                         walk in, cross to bar.)

MARY

Look, two more pigeons.

SAMANTHA

I want Delbert! And by gawd I'm gonna get that low-
down muscleman to bend his knee begging me for
marriage.

MARY

You can afford to wait. You're birthday's next
month. I have to move now, today, pronto.

SAMANTHA

Oh, what's a day?

                         (Mary takes deep breath, lights
                         cigarette, coughs up phlegm, spits on
                         floor.)

MARY

I could be dead by tomorrow! On my tombstone it had
better say, Mrs. not Miss.

SAMANTHA

By then nobody would care.

(Mary mimics women walking by her
tombstone, pointing sadly.)

MARY
(mimics four different women)
"Oh, dear. Look at this poor soul. She was an
unmarried woman." "She was a sinner." "A bloody
prostitute I bet." "I bet she's glad she's dead.

(Samantha intervenes, hugs Mary.)

SAMANTHA
It's not that bad, Mary. You're overreacting.

(Mary mimics woman, points to a grave,
bends low, wipes dirt from stone.)

MARY
(mimics four different women)
"Oooh, what do we have here? My gosh, Miss Samantha
Petunia Panther died of a broken heart, alone and
banished from society. The poor thing." "Don't you
feel sorry for that bitch. All she wanted was fun
in life." "She didn't want the responsibility to
raise a family." "A dirty tramp that deserved to
die for the exotic life she lived."

SAMANTHA
That does it!

(Samantha races to bar, leaps on one of
the two men standing by the bar.)

SAMANTHA
(continuing)
Where have you been all my life, you big hunk?

(Mary tackles the other man to floor,
ripping at his clothes)

(TWO WOMEN enter, gasp in horror.)

FIRST WOMAN
Get off my husband.

SECOND WOMAN
You cheating sons-of-bitches.

FIRST MAN
Darling!

SECOND MAN
I'm innocent!

(Two women pull Samantha and Mary off.)

                         SAMANTHA
     (to first woman)
You should be grateful.

                         FIRST WOMAN

Grateful? For what?

                         MARY

We're virgins.

                         SAMANTHA

Exactly.

                         MARY

Postulants. We left the convent for acting career.

                         SECOND WOMAN

For sex acts.

                         SAMANTHA

To induce a challenge. We're testing your
husbands's fidelity. You should be thankful.

                         MARY

Believe me. You married women need gals like us.

                              (They step aside as old friends, chit-
                              chatting. Husbands stare nervously.
                              Samantha whispers.)

                              (Two women race back, slap husbands,
                              grab their ears and exit, OW! OW!)

                         FIRST HUSBAND
Honest, darling. I don't know them.

                         SECOND HUSBAND
Oh, sugarbuns. Be merciful.

                              (Samantha and Mary high-five.)

                         SAMANTHA

Two down, more to go.
                              (They scan the bar. MEN rise and
                              leave.)

                         MARY

Get back here!

                         SAMANTHA

Let'em go, babe.
                              (They sit on couch.)

                         MARY
     (yells)
Where's the bloody waitress? I want a drink.

                        SAMANTHA
Service! Service, please!

                                (Waitress with tray delivers two
                                drinks, turns to walk away.)

                        MARY
     (sternly)
All of them.
     (beat)
Spoiled bitch.

                                (Waitress slams tray on coffee table,
                                angrily leaves.)

                        SAMANTHA
Who does she think she is?

                        MARY
She's married.

                        SAMANTHA
So what?

                        MARY
Gives her the right to be a bitch.

                                (They guzzle drinks. Spill drinks to
                                floor.)

                        MARY
     (continuing)
Waitress! Clean up this mess.

                                (Waitress arrives, wipes floor.)

                        SAMANTHA
How long you been married?

                        WAITRESS
Too long.

                        MARY
It shows. Look at your fat butt. You can thank
your husband for that monstrosity clinging to you
like an evil demon. Your boobs dangle with nowhere
to go. Look what he did to your face--

                                (Waitress cries, sits down.)

                        WAITRESS
I wish I was never married. It ruined my figure.

                                (Samantha listens intently.)

                         WAITRESS
     (continuing; sobbing)
Life was a rose garden when I was single. I thought
marriage was the right thing to do. You know? All
my friends were married and had children. I
couldn't bear the scorn.
     (mimics people talking)
"Look at Delores, she's a fair maiden with nobody to
spend the night." "A nymphomaniac can bear no
husband." "Such a sinful woman she is."

                         (Samantha and Mary laugh.)

                         SAMANTHA
Delores, people don't say those things.

                         MARY
Ahh, it's all in your mind.

                         DELORES
It's true, they do. See those two gals over there?

                         (Delores points to TWO WOMEN sitting at
                         bar.)

                         DELORES
     (continuing)
I heard them talking about you.

              SAMANTHA   MARY
            Noooo!   Noooo!

                         DELORES
It's true. Gossip is a killer for single women.
That's why you don't have husbands. Married women
are jealous and they gossip, spreading lies, just so
they can perpetuate the gossip.

                         (Samantha and Mary storm to the two
                         women, yank them from chairs, grasp
                         collars.)

                         SAMANTHA
Talking nasty 'bout us, huh?

                         MARY
Married bitches.

                         (Delores laughs loudly.)

                         (Two women reveal badges, arrest
                         Samantha and Mary.)

                         MARY
     (continuing; to Delores)
I'll get you for this.

                          DELORES
Good luck. I'm going to South America with my
husband.

                              (Delores rips off apron, exits.)

                          MARY
You creepy married gossiping no good--

                        SAMANTHA
I don't want a husband!

                      FIRST WOMAN
Okay, come along now.

                              (Place cuffs on them.)

                          MARY
Ow! It's cold.

                        SAMANTHA
Get them things off my hands, you broke my nail!

                              (Out they go. Everyone in bar breathes
                              a sigh of relief.)

        CURTAIN FALLS.

     (END OF SCENE B)

ACT II

SCENE C

    SETTING: NIGHT CLUB

    AT RISE:

                              (Delbert and Simon enter, dressed in
                              formal coat and tie. Club is vacant.)

                      SIMON
They're gone.
                      DELBERT
Like whispering ghosts on a breezy summer eve,
they'll magically materialize out of thin air.

                              (Samantha and Mary secretly enter, duck
                              behind bar, listening.)

                              (Delbert and Simon pour beer and sit on
                              couch.)

                         SIMON
I'm not sure about this, Delbert.
                              (Delbert gags on beer, wipes mouth.)

                         SIMON
      (continuing)
Sorry 'bout that, Delbert. Look, maybe those chicks
are not clucking.

                         DELBERT
Will you shut up for once? All chicks cluck.

                              (Sam and Mary's heads pop up, looking
                              mean. Delbert and Simon light
                              cigarettes.)

                         SIMON
I don't know about these two birds. I heard a rumor
once that if you try too hard to get a girl they can
sense your desperation like body odor.

                              (Delbert removes cologne from pocket,
                              sprays Simon's body.)

                         DELBERT
Here! Sniff!

                         SIMON
I'm serious.

                         DELBERT
So am I, now shut up so I can think.

                         SIMON
You like the one with the big--

                         DELBERT
Shut-up!
                         SIMON
Aha, so the truth arises from the ashes of despair.
The lonely heart reflects upon the face.

                         DELBERT
You're nuts. Okay, she's got nice bazoomers. If
you're lonely, just go to San Francisco, bend over
and tie your shoelaces... you understand the meaning
of this?

                              (Samantha's mixed up, points to
                              breasts. Mary nods. Samantha grins,
                              bats her eyes.)

                         DELBERT
      (continuing)
And big wide muffins. Did you see her waddle when
she walks?
                         SIMON
Quack! Quack!

                              (Both laugh. Samantha stares coldly,
                              checks her buns.)

                    DELBERT
And Mary. Ha! She's a bad girl, Simon.

                              (Mary's upset, stares coldly.)

                    SIMON
I want a bad girl. I don't want some prim bitch who
believes she's the Queen of Sheeba.

                    DELBERT
Sheeba? You mean the Miss Mademoiselle herself.

                              (Mary feels better, gloats in her
                              glory.)

                    SIMON
Yeah, yeah. She's a royal sophisticated woman.
Cleopatra properties I tell ya. A very decent girl.

                              (Samantha frowns as Mary radiates.)

                    DELBERT
Don't let her good looks fool you, Simon.
Underneath the tons of powder, glue, paint, and
sprays she's a sex-starved horny woman just like,
Samantha.

                              (Samantha and Mary boiling mad.)

                    DELBERT
     (continuing)
And I'll tell you another thing or two about those
glorious feminine itches.

                    SIMON
I don't want to hear it, you're talking drunk.

                    DELBERT
Well you're going to. Don't ever marry women. I
tell you, don't buy the cow, the milk is free, man.

                              (Simon and Delbert laugh. Samantha and
                              Mary grab whiskey bottles, chug on
                              them. Wipe lips like gunslingers.)

                    DELBERT
     (continuing)
What the hell do you want to get married for anyway?
Everyone we know who did is a sorry fool for doing
it. Look at us, we're free... and happy.

                              (Both stare with drunk expressions.)

                              SIMON
I remember reading in the bible it's not good for
man to be alone.

                              DELBERT
You're not alone, Simon.

                                        (Simon stares with shock. Samantha and
                                        Mary's chins sink, eyes expand.)

                              SIMON
Oh, no. I like women.

                              DELBERT
So do I, Simon.

                                        (Delbert pats Simon's knee. Simon
                                        freezes, stares with fright.)

                              DELBERT
      (continuing)
Now what's bugging you?

                              SIMON
I thought you were, were, ah--

                              DELBERT
You A-hole! I said you're not alone. Look, a man
is a perfect creature--

                                        (Samantha and Mary frown scornfully.
                                        Fingers in mouth, pretend to gag.)

                              DELBERT
      (continuing)
... he is self-contained. Adam didn't need a woman.
He had himself and all the animals in Eden to
satisfy his needs. I mean, food was everywhere
without a fight.

                              SIMON
Ahh, I see. It was a peaceful world.

                              DELBERT
Paradise, Simon. Pure unadulterated paradise. If
God wanted women he would have made them first...
man was meant to be alone.
      (child-like)
... but Adam had to bitch and the bitch came forth.

                                        (Delbert tosses napkin to floor.
                                        Samantha attempts to fetch it. Mary
                                        restrains her.)

                              DELBERT
      (continuing)
Listen. You don't hear it do you?

> (Simon turns head. Samantha and Mary
> momentarily duck.)

                    SIMON

Hear what?

                    DELBERT
     (imitates female voice)
Pick that up! I'm not going to put up with your
slobby manners. I just cleaned the floor.

> (Samantha and Mary light cigarettes.
> Stare intently.)

                    SIMON

Yeah, paradise. To be a man. To live like a man.
To do what a man really wants to do... nothing.

                    DELBERT

Right on, nothing. But ol' Adam was a whining wimp,
always complaining, blaming the animals for this and
that. You know what really drove him nuts? Monkeys!

                    SIMON

Monkeys?

> (Simon gags on his drink.)

                    DELBERT

Yep, monkeys. They tore up the place, leaving
banana peels, apple cores, papaya skins and
pomegranate seeds everywhere.

                    SIMON

It makes sense. God saw the mess.

                    DELBERT

Yep. Blamed it on Adam. You know what Adam said?
It's in the Bible.

                    SIMON

Get rid of the monkeys?

                    DELBERT

No, Bozo. Adam stood tall and said, "I've got a
world to run. I don't have time for picking up all
this trash."

> (Delbert tosses napkin to floor.
> Samantha moves for it. Mary puts her
> in a head-lock. They struggle.)

                    SIMON

He argued with God?

                        DELBERT
Adam may have been wimpy, but he stood his ground
when it came to picking up trash and stuff.
Cleaning just wasn't his program. Like us, he
refused to defile himself with such menial chores.

                        SIMON
You mean to tell me God makes mistakes?

                              (Samantha and Mary nod heads as Delbert
                              wags his.)

                        DELBERT
No, Simon. God doesn't make mistakes. He knows the
future. He knew Adam would betray him.

                        SIMON
So what happens next?

                        DELBERT
Don't you ever read the bible?

                              (Simon wags head.)

                        DELBERT
     (continuing)
Well, God then said, "Adam, you ruined my paradise
I set forth for you. I will make you a helper,
someone to clean up this awful place."

                              (Samantha and Mary frown, hands on
                              hips.)

                        SIMON
Wow! God was cool to let Adam off the hook so
easily. I would have thrashed him for messing up my
paradise.

                              (Mary wags a fist at Simon. Samantha
                              stares coldly, lips pursed.)

                        DELBERT
Now you get it? Women were made to pick up after
us. To tend to our needs. God made a little slave
girl for Adam.

                              (Samantha and Mary lip-speak, "Slave
                              girl?")

                        SIMON
Imaging that! I like this God of the Bible. He's
cool.

                        DELBERT
If you pray to him, he will give you a little slave
girl too.

                    (Samantha and Mary reveal razor sharp
                    teeth.)

                         SIMON
     (prays)
Oh, God of paradise, Adam's friend. Cast upon me
thy servant so I may live a life at ease. And teach
thee maiden to never say no to me.

                         DELBERT
Be careful for what you pray for. You just may get
it.

                         SIMON
I want a wife so I can go about and live my life.
My apartment's a mess. I don't have time to clean
it, wash my clothes, cook, etc. Like you always
said, Delbert, it's a woman's duty to cater to a
man's needs. I got to pee.

                              (Simon and Delbert rise, Samantha and
                              Mary duck behind bar as Delbert and
                              Simon exit to restroom.)

                         MARY
Them no good s.o.b's. Telling horrid stories like
that. We are women! Not slaves! We are not
magnets destined to gathering clothes, make the
beds, cook, pick up after a man and bear children.
We have a greater purpose in life.

                              (Samantha picks up napkins on floor,
                              wipes table.)

                         MARY
     (continuing)
Don't you pick up after them.

                              (Samantha catches herself, thinks.)

                         SAMANTHA
Play it on. Play it on. I'm telling you these two
are the fools we've been praying for.

                              (They hear voices and footsteps and
                              duck back behind the bar.)

                              (Simon falls to his knees.)

                         DELBERT
Wait! I haven't finished the story--

                         SIMON
     (prays)
Oh hear my cry, oh, Lord. Bring forth my servant to
be.

                              (Mary and Samantha step to F. All
                              smiles.)

                         SIMON
     (continuing)
My prayers have been answered!

                         DELBERT
I think they have.

                         SAMANTHA
Aren't you going to offer us a drink?

                         DELBERT
Sure, would you like a drink?

                              (Mary and Samantha nod.)

                         DELBERT
     (continuing)
Simon?

                                   (Simon nods.)

                         DELBERT
     (continuing)
Well, there you have it. Simon's thirsty.

                              (Simon rubs his parched throat.)

                         DELBERT
     (continuing)
Well? You're not going to let a man die of thirst
are you?

                              (Samantha and Mary take Delbert and
                              Simon's glasses to bar, fill with beer
                              and return.)

                         SIMON
Thank you my precious.

                              (Mary swoons hearing those words.
                              Samantha delivers drink to Delbert.)

                         DELBERT
My love. You are so kind.
                               (Samantha bats her eyes. Delbert looks
                              away, face into beer.)

                              (Just as they drink, Samantha and Mary
                              slap the drinks spilling it on them and
                              barge into ladies room.)

               SIMON   DELBERT
     Hey!   What's going on here?

(Delbert and Simon stand soaked.)

                    SIMON
I thought God answered my prayers?

                    DELBERT
He did, fool. You didn't let me finish the story.
Once he made Eve, she became his tormenter!

                    SIMON
Oh, nooo!

                    DELBERT
And let me tell you one more thing. Don't ever give
a woman an apple, or a beer.

                    SIMON
I won't, Delbert. I promise. Who told you 'bout
these things?

                    DELBERT
Bud.

                    SIMON
Bud? Bud who?

                    DELBERT
Budweiser, stupid.

                    (Simon and Delbert exit R.)

                    (Samantha and Mary enter.)

                    MARY
Wouldn't you know it? They ran away.

                    SAMANTHA
Chickens.

                    MARY
We need another method. This definitely isn't
working. I'm incredibly desperate, Sam. I only
have one day left.

                    SAMANTHA
Hold your horses, Mrs. Ben Hur. The race has hardly
begun. You still have tomorrow.

                    (Mary gasps.)

                    MARY
I could die in my sleep.

                    SAMANTHA
Trust me, I've got it all planned.

MARY

But what if they don't like us? I mean, we can't
make men marry us that don't like us. Can we?

SAMANTHA

Tsk, Mary, Mary, Mary. Every girl we know forced
the man to marry them. Men don't leap up and down
saying, "Let's get married, darling, so I can work
my butt off the rest of my rotten life supporting
you." Oh, no. We use stealth strategies, darling.
Make them feel like they must marry us to make us
happy.

MARY

Sort of like, if they make us happy by marrying
them, we in turn will make them very, very, happy?

SAMANTHA

Exactly.

MARY

I don't get it. How do we do that by spilling
drinks on them?

(Samantha paces.)

SAMANTHA

No wonder you're not married, Mary. Haven't you
been listening to the sermons in the ladies rooms
all your life?

(Mary's confounded. Both light
cigarettes.)

SAMANTHA
(continuing)
That's our college, darling! It's the institute of
higher education where wisdom resides. Why do you
think girls all think the same way? You assume
we're born this way?

(Mary nods, grins.)

SAMANTHA
(continuing)
And you thought the pyramids were King's burial
chambers? It was the Egyption's ladies room! It
stands for eternity proclaiming our glorious
heritage and triumph over mankind.

(Samantha gazes to heaven.)

SAMANTHA
(continuing; gazes to heaven)
Oh, Cleopatra. High priestess of glamour.
Trailblazing our path to glory. Wisest of them all.

MARY

Then why was she bitten by a snake?

SAMANTHA

How was she supposed to know a snake was creeping in
the basket of chestnuts?

MARY

Her ex-husband?

SAMANTHA

Exactly. Ceasar didn't die. It's a lie. A bloody
lie he made up to cover-up his own sins. That's
another story. Look, I know what I'm doing. You
got to play tough with these boys or they won't be
stimulated.

MARY

I could stimulate them with these.

                    (Mary gyrates hips. Bartender enters,
                    claps hands. Mary's embarrassed.)

BARTENDER

Nice show.

SAMANTHA

She was practicing her steps.

                    (Mary and Samantha practice dance
                    steps.)

                    (People arrive, bar fills up.
                    Discjockey slips on music. Samantha
                    and Mary sit at couch, pouting.)

SAMANTHA
    (continuing)
Look sorrowful, darling. Men perceive lonely women
are easy pickup's.

                    (Samantha moves coffee table with foot
                    to form a walkway.)

                    (Men notice, pass right on by. Mary
                    extends foot, trips one. He falls on
                    her. Mary bear-hugs him, kissing.)

                    (Samantha extends leg, men sidestep.
                    She's fuming mad. Races to bar, grabs
                    a man's drink, guzzles it down.)

                    (Samantha forces the man to slow dance.)

                    (Delbert and Simon enter R., shocked.)

DELBERT
Typical women. One minute they love you, the next
they're making it on with another man.

SIMON
Yeah. I'm telling God I changed my mind. I rather
be single.

DELBERT
We don't want women like that anyway.

SIMON
Nope.

                    (Simon races over to Mary, pulls her
                    away from the man.)

                    (Delbert breaks into the dance.)

SIMON
    (continuing)
Mary! How could you?

MARY
He tripped and fell--

SIMON
On your lips?

SAMANTHA
    (to Simon)
Leave her alone! She can't control gravity!

DELBERT
And what's your excuse?

SAMANTHA
Excuse? I don't need an excuse. I'm not married to
you. And believe you me, you are not my type.

                    (Samantha crosses to bar, grabs another
                    man's drink. Man fights for it.
                    Samantha bends his finger backward,
                    guzzles it down. Hugs him.)

SAMANTHA
    (continuing; looking over shoulder at Delbert)
Thank you, dar..ling.

MAN
Ow! Ow! Let go.

                    (Samantha pecks him on cheek. Delbert
                    frowns. Samantha smiles.)
                    (Mary slaps Simon. Samantha prances up
                    to Delbert, all smiles, slaps him.)

MARY   SAMANTHA

That's for watching us.   That's for watching us.

> (Delbert and Simon are dumfounded.
> Samantha and Mary storm into ladies
> room.)

SIMON

I don't get it? What's going on here?

DELBERT

I think we're in trouble.

SIMON

Trouble? What kind of trouble?

DELBERT

I think these gals are ex-convicts. They are
playing a game on us, Simon.

SIMON

Convicts? Murderers?

DELBERT

Could be. They are not acting right at all. They
got it in for us.

SIMON

        (looks to heaven, prays)
Oh, God. Take them away. I promise you I'll be
good.

DELBERT

We better get out of here, and fast.

> (They exit, but are intercepted by
> Samantha and Mary, firm grips on their
> collars.)

SAMANTHA

Going somewhere, boys?

MARY

Skipping out on the town without us?

DELBERT

Look. We've had it with your games. No more.
Enough of the bullpoop.

MARY

You sound so ungrateful to have a hot date, babe.

SIMON

You're ex-convicts. Aren't you?
> (Samantha and Mary laugh.)

                          SAMANTHA
Convicts? You must be kidding?
     (to Mary)
Convicts! Ha! These boys have imagination.

                           MARY
     (to Samantha)
And fine bodies to pilfer too. Don't blow this, Sam.
     (desperate)
I need a husband.

          SIMON   DELBERT
        Husband?   Husband?

                          SAMANTHA
She was just asking if you were husbands. Are you?

                           MARY
I don't fondle married men.

                          DELBERT
Ah, so you gal's are soiled doves?

                              (Samantha and Mary's feet stomp floor
                               BOOM!)

          MARY   SAMANTHA
        We are virgins! How dare   We are virgins! How dare
        you?   you?

                          DELBERT
Oh, I beg my pardon.

                           MARY
Then get on your knees and repent.

                          SAMANTHA
It's time we tell you the truth. We are Sisters of
Mercy.

                          SIMON
Nuns? That explains their violent nature.

                          DELBERT
What do you mean, sisters? And what do you mean,
mercy?

                           MARY
I've got to pee.

Hold on a minute, now. Not so fast.

                          SAMANTHA
Leave her alone, she has no bladder! She lost it in
the war!

                          DELBERT
She likely fell off a bar stool or a sailor's
bunkbed.

                          SIMON
     (to Mary)
You were in the military?

                                   (Mary's confused. Samantha nods.)

                          SAMANTHA
Marine Corps. She was a Marine. Tell'em, Mary.

                          MARY
I was on them, in them, after them.
     (yells)
I served my country!

                          SAMANTHA
She means she was on duty, in the line of fire and
came after those who were wounded. Like a Sister of
Mercy.

                                   (Mary nods.)

                          MARY
Now may I pee?

                                   (Mary exits to ladies room. Samantha
                                   follows.)

                          DELBERT
Why do you have to go at the same time she does?

                          SAMANTHA
A woman can never be left alone in the ladies room.
One never knows what evil lurks behind those stalls.
There could be a pervert hiding inside and--

                          DELBERT
Go, go, go. My ears are full of it already.

                                   (Delbert covers ears with hands. Wags
                                   head.)

                                   (Samantha and Mary enter ladies room.)

                                   (Simon pulls Delbert's hands down.)

                          SIMON
That explains everything, Delbert. It explains why
they are acting so strange. They are, virgins! I
never had a virgin before. Gosh, I want one.
Imagine telling mom, "Hey, mum! I got a virgin.
You were wrong, ma. They are not mythical
creatures."

(Delbert slaps Simon on the head.)

DELBERT
Don't you dare tell your mother anything about us
chasing skirts. I don't want her here.

(Simon's mother, Gertrude, enters.)

GERTRUDE
Simon? Simon? Where the hell are you, Simon?

DELBERT
Oh, brother. I ought to ring your face out.

SIMON
I had to tell her.

GERTRUDE
Darling, sugarplum. I've been looking all over town
for you.
    (glances at Delbert)
I see you are still hanging out with this awful man.

SIMON
Mother, don't start a scene.

GERTRUDE
Why? You have girls around? Is that it, Simon?
Chasing skirts again?

SIMON
Yes, mom.

(Gertrude pinches his ear, pulls him to
F.)

GERTRUDE
How many times must I tell you? You will never find
a nice girl in bar rooms.

SIMON
I don't want a nice girl, ma.

(Delbert laughs. Gertrude kicks him in
shin. Ouch!)

(Mary and Samantha enter, freeze, smile
at what they see.)

GERTRUDE
    (pulls Simon to exit)
Simon, you get home right now. I sense danger in
the air.

(Mary and Samantha intercept.)

SAMANTHA

What's this? Mama?

GERTRUDE

Who are these floozies? Simon? These are not the
type of women you want to marry.

MARY

What's it gonna be, Simon. Mamma tucking you in, or
me and you having a night on the town?

GERTRUDE

I'm his mother and don't you interfere with our
relationship.
     (to Simon, sulking)
Is this the woman who will take my place? If so, I
may as well check myself into the nursing home and
patiently wait for Dr. Kervorkian to arrive with his
little bag of needles.
     (beat)
After all I've done for you, Simon. And this is how
you reward your mother? The gift of death.

                    SIMON

Stop it, ma.

                         (Samantha whispers in Getrude's ear.)

GERTRUDE

Ohhh! I didn't know. Mary? Sister Mary, Mary?
You're a nun? Oh, I beg my pardon. Wait, where is
your habit?
                    MARY

     (stumbled)
I still have my bad habits.

SAMANTHA

She means, she doesn't wear the old habits. This is
the New Age. Doesn't she look angelic?

DELBERT

Now wait a minute here. What's the meaning of all
this? One minute she's a virgin, the next a
marine, and now a nun.

GERTRUDE

Don't you talk to Sister Mary, Mary like that, you,
you, sinner!

                         (Samantha pushes Mary's hands into
                         prayer.)

DELBERT

I don't know what you women are up to, but I'll get
to the bottom of this yet. And if I uncover you're
dirty deeds I'll call the Pope myself and toss you
into the arena, where you both belong. Understand
the meaning of this?

                        (Delbert storms to bar.)

                        MARY
That no good son-of-a --

                        SAMANTHA
Sinner. Let us pray for him.

                              (Mary frowns. Samantha pulls Mary down
                              as she kneels.)

                        SAMANTHA
     (continuing)
Shut off the music! It's time to pray for that very
sinful man standing at the bar. His name is,
Delbert and he'll go to hell if we don't save him
now!

                              (Everyone stares at Delbert. His eyes
                              roll up. Everyone silent. Gertrude
                              forces Simon to kneel.)

                              (Samantha elbows Mary.)

                        SAMANTHA
     (continuing)
Pray.

                        MARY
I don't know how to pray.

                              (Gertrude beads eyes suspiciously.)

                        SAMANTHA
She doesn't know the words to say,
     (looks over shoulder, yells to Delbert)
...for such a sinful man that he is.

                        MARY
     (her prayer)
Oh, heaven's of mercy, I beg you to find me a --

                        SAMANTHA
Word to say. Word to say.

                        MARY
Word to say for such a sinner that I know--

                        SAMANTHA
He is.

                        MARY
That I know he is.

                                SAMANTHA
                    (to Gertrude)
                She flunked prayer meditation classes. Most saint's
                do, did you know that? They are above all us
                mortals. So centered in the spirit. We often
                misinterpret their prayers.

                                MARY
                And if I ever get my hands on that S.O.B. --

                                SAMANTHA
                    (to Gertrude)
                S.O.B. short for Son of Beelzebub.

                                MARY
                -- I'll kick him in the rump and deliver him to hell
                myself. Amen.

                                CROWD
                Amen!

                                    (They rise. Gertrude hugs Mary. Mary
                                    winces in pain. SFX ribs cracking.)

                                MARY
                Ow! You're crushing my ribs.

                                SAMANTHA
                She hasn't begun martyrdom training, yet. Next week.

                                    (Mary nods, rubs her ribs.)

                                GERTRUDE
                My, the church sure has changed since I was a little
                girl.
                    (to Simon)
                Now you keep your hands off Sister Mary. You hear
                me, boy? I'll be watching you. I have spies, you
                know?

                                SIMON
                Yes, mother.

                                GERTRUDE
                    (to Mary)
                He would have made a fine monk, but worldly
                pleasures perverted his mind.

                                    (Gertrude genuflects, kisses Mary's
                                    hand, crosses to exit.)

                                GERTRUDE
                    (continuing; to Delbert)
                Stay away from my son... you unrepentant sinner!
                I'm telling your mother!

CROWD

Sinner!

DELBERT

Gertrude? Gertrude? Wait, please. Don't tell my
mother nothing!

                    (Gertrude storms out. Delbert wags
                    head, runs out. Simon follows.
                    Music plays.)

MARY

Now what the hell was that all about, huh? Simon
won't marry me now. He can't. His mother thinks
I'm a nun. You screwed-up this one, Sam.

SAMANTHA

I suppose I did. I can still get a man.

MARY

You can? For me?

SAMANTHA

No. Me.

MARY

     (yells)
What about me?

SAMANTHA

We'll have to find a way to excommunicate you from
the church so you will be worthy to marry, Simon.

MARY

What church? I'm not in a cathedral. You're
confusing me.

SAMANTHA

I'm confusing you? First, for your information, bar
rooms are holy places. Miracles happen here.
Fantasies can become reality, darling. Secondly,
you're the one that's so damn desperate for a
husband you had me kneeling in prayer. Look what
you've done! Flat knees.

                    (Samantha walks knock-kneed. Mary walks
                    likewise.)

MARY

I can't help it, I'm not a nun. I just want a man.

                    (They exit.)

CROWD

Good riddance!

                    (Music turns up, people dance fast.)

                              (Samantha and Mary poke heads from
                              doorway. Bartender shoos them away.)

                              BARTENDER
Out! Out! Come back when you've learned manners.

                              MARY
How dare you!

                                   (Bartender wags head, crosses to bar.
                                   Gertrude enters with a priest. Music
                                   stops, people freeze.)

                              PRIEST
It's okay, go ahead. Just keep your hands where
they should be, unless your married.

                                   (Men and ladies slip on rings, wave
                                   hands in air. Music plays at lower
                                   volume.)

                              GERTRUDE
Well, father. She was here a moment ago.

                              PRIEST
I can tell you this, my dear. I had better not find
a nun in a bar. You said sexy clothes, huh?

                              GERTRUDE
Smashing lady I must say she was. She seemed very
religious, father. She had that angelic glow.

                              PRIEST
The devil comes in many disguises.
     (to crowd, yells)
Anyone need a confession? My hours are three p.m.
Wednesday and Saturday.

                                   (He passes out business cards, then
                                   leaves with Gertrude.)

                              MAN
     (to Bartender)
What in tarnation is going on here? First we have
two dingbats moronic ladies, prayer meetings, a
priest, what's next?

                              (Two clowns enter.)

                              MAN
     (continuing)
This can't be happening.

                              BARTENDER
     (to clowns)
Out! Out! We're full. I'm sorry. Out!

                              (Clowns frown.)

                         WOMAN
Get out!

                              (Clowns extend tongues and leave.)

                       BARTENDER
I quit! I'm selling this joint once and for all.

                         WOMAN
Wait, don't quit. We need you.

                       BARTENDER
I'm losing my sanity. I'm choosing another line of
work. I can't take it anymore.

                              (Bartender holds his head as he exits,
                              mumbling like a babbling idiot.)

                              (Bartender returns, backing up. Two
                              cops with the two clowns.)

                       FIRST CLOWN
     (disguised voice)
That's the culprit, officer.

                       SECOND CLOWN
     (disguised voice)
It's discrimination I tell you.

                       FIRST COP
Well? What gives?

                       BARTENDER
I've had a long day. Okay, they can stay.

                              (Everyone gets up and exits. Cops
                              leave. Clowns sit and stare coldly at
                              bartender as he serves them drinks at
                              a table.)

                       FIRST CLOWN
You think a clown leads an easy life? Well they
don't. It's the likes of your kind that makes it
unbearable.

                       SECOND CLOWN
Drives us to drink.

                              (First clown rises, heads to ladies
                              room.)

                       BARTENDER
Hey? That's the ladies room.

                       SECOND CLOWN
Leave her alone!

                              (First clown enters ladies room.)

                              BARTENDER
Her? Hey! Your those stupid bitches I told to
leave. You're bankrupting me!

                              (Samantha exits in clown outfit.)

                              SAMANTHA
Look, buddy ol' pal. We are on a critical mission.

                              (Samantha and Mary whip out F.B.I. I.D.
                              cards.)

                              BARTENDER
F.B.I.? Well, that explains this zany activity.
What's going on? Am I in trouble?

                              MARY
You may be.

                              SAMANTHA
Shush, lower your voice. We're here to protect you.

                              BARTENDER
Protect me? From who?

            MARY   SAMANTHA
        The mob!   The mob!

                              BARTENDER
The mob? I don't--

                              SAMANTHA
Shhh! The place may be bugged. You have enemies.
That man, Wicked Pete? He's been identified as
Marcellus Ruckus --

                              MARY
Granddaddy of the Italian Texas Longhorn mob. Those
two guys we've been tailgating, Simon and Delbert?

                              SAMANTHA
Hit men. Chicago wise-guys. Hard-core killers.

                              (Bartender sinks into a chair.)

                              BARTENDER
What am I going to do? Why? Why me?

                              MARY
The mob has reasons. That's what we're here for, to
find out.
                              SAMANTHA
All you have to do is obey us. We'll be on the
scene when they make their move.

                              MARY
It's important that you act natural.

SAMANTHA
That means if you were rude to us before, stay that
way. Don't let them on you know. Understand?

BARTENDER
Why? Why? I don't associate with the mob.

SAMANTHA
That's likely why. They need laundromats to wash
money. They kill you and simply take over the
place. It's done all the time.

BARTENDER
I could skip out of the country.

                    (Mary and Samantha laugh.)

MARY
Where? To Sicily? Columbia? Russia?

BARTENDER
France. I'll go to France.

SAMANTHA
Right, the French Connection will cement you to the
bottom of the Thames River.

BARTENDER
That's in London.

MARY
No kidding. It's a French tradition. With two-
dozen bridges, Thames is a perfect disposal site.
Don't argue with us.

SAMANTHA
You go home, as usual. We'll stay here for the
night looking for bugs.

                    (Bartender leaves. Mary and Samantha
                    giggle. Cross to bar, pour and sip
                    Snakebite whiskey drinks. Both
                    momentarily reveal fangs and hiss.)

SAMANTHA
   (continuing)
Damn good stuff. Nothing like a good snakebite to
start the day. If more women drank this stuff there
would be less single men running around bugging us
women, I tell you.

                    (Samantha swings fist mimicking hitting
                    man on chin.)

MARY
You're right, Sam. Men are so gullible. They
believe us women.

                    (Mary screams, sees a bug crawling,
                    kicks bar.)

                    SAMANTHA
They better believe us or they will get no sex. Not
from me. I demand unadulterated honesty in a
relationship... even if he is married.

                              (Mary sprays floor with insecticide.
                              They drink heavily.)

                    MARY
I hate bugs. Why do they follow me like they do?

                              (Samantha smirks.)

                    SAMANTHA
You're a buggery little gal. There's remarkable
similarities between a man and an insect, both will
bug a woman just to piss us off.

                              (They Tug-O-War the insecticide can.
                              Mary wins, stuffs it in pocket book.)

                    MARY
This is getting deep, Sam. I'm not so sure it could
backfire on us.

                              (They both light cigarettes.)

                    SAMANTHA
It's all for love, babe. A woman must use every
dirty trick she can to snag a man. Men will not
walk down that isle willingly. If we must use
extortion, deception, fraud, misrepresentation, we
use it. Marriage is serious business, and I'm dead
serious.
     (drunk, fists clenched, screams)
I'll kill the man who say's no to me.

                    MARY
I'm determined too, Sam. But we might be going to
far.

                    SAMANTHA
Too far? This isn't nothing, Mary. Nothing
compared to what other people do. Look at President
Clinton. Lovely Hillery had to hook into the
Whitewater deal for him to say, "I do." What
about --

                    MARY
Oh, all right. I understand. But if we end up in
prison it's going to be your fault.

                    SAMANTHA
That's okay. I'll visit you when I can.

MARY

Visit me?

SAMANTHA

Well, somebody's got to take the rap.

MARY

Deals off. I'm not doing it.

SAMANTHA

Oh, be that way then. Never mind, see if I care if
you end up an old lady with a barren womb and
grotesque knuckles to show for your life.

                    (Samantha crumples her hands resembling
                    arthritis. Mary flips cigarette to
                    floor.)

MARY

I'll get arthritis anyway, man or no man.

SAMANTHA

Look at your skin. Your face already has laugh
lines. You know why they call them that don't you?
Because men laugh at us for getting old and ugly
once you hit thirty.

                    (Mary covers her ears.)

SAMANTHA
      (continuing)
That's right, thir-ty!

                     (Samantha rises, mimics old lady
                     walking with cane.)

SAMANTHA
      (continuing; gravely voice)
My name is, Mary. I was once a beautiful fox living
a life of true glamour. Oh, if I could only go back
and change the past, I would have listened to my
dear friend, Samantha. Now she has a rich husband
and looks wonderful.

                    (Mary's hands still cover ears.)

MARY

I don't hear anything... a rich husband you say?

SAMANTHA

Certainly. Behind every success is a failed husband
with a successful wife. It's how presidents and
movie stars are made, honey. If it weren't for us
women, no man would make it in this world. The lazy
brutes!

MARY

I've always wanted to be rich. Simon and Delbert
are struggling actors too --

                              SAMANTHA
But if we make them rich they will have to marry us.
You'll be dripping in diamonds. The envy of all
jealous women. Do you understand the meaning of
this?

                                MARY
What are you scheming now? Nothing has worked so
far. Why can't we just get a man like we used to?
Slip a pill in their drinks and... whoopie!

                              SAMANTHA
Pills wear off, darling. And they get pissed off
when they find out.

                                MARY
Bunch of poor sports.

                              SAMANTHA
At your age, honey... it is imperative to use every
trick in the book of womanhood passed down to us
from the ages.
     (gazes to heaven)
Ohhh, thank you, Cleopatra, Diana, Venus, Athena and
Mars.

                                MARY
Mars? The God of war?

                              SAMANTHA
This is warfare, it's a matter of survival. We must
snag husbands or forever pay the price. All is fair
in love and war, sweetcheeks.

                                        (Samantha crosses to bar, scans want
                                        ads, moves to F. with drinks in hand.)

                                MARY
Sam? You didn't?

                                        (Samantha hands a drink to Mary.)

                              SAMANTHA
Look at all these women advertising for lovers.
     (reads ad)
"Easygoing, kind, honest, intelligent.
     (to Mary)
Nobody wants an intelligent woman.

             SAMANTHA   MARY
             Nobody!   Nobody!

                              SAMANTHA
Look at this ad.
     (reads another ad)
"Adventurous beauty, attractive, adorable, honest,
vibrant woman, seeks her dream gentleman.

MARY

No such animal, babe. No wonder she's running ads.

(Samantha flips pages.)

SAMANTHA

Where's the men section. Look-it, look-it this.
     (reads ad)
"Two lovable actors seek two sassy fabulous mature
women with a sense of humor."
     (to Mary)
That's us, Mary!

(Mary snatches paper, her hands
vibrate, drink spilling.)

MARY

     (reads ad)
"Must love cooking, washing clothes, housecleaning."
     (to Samantha)
What is this trash?

SAMANTHA

Give that to me.

(Samantha snatches paper. They Tug-O-
War, it rips in two.)

MARY

Now look what you've done?

(Samantha puts pieces together, but
they don't line up.)

SAMANTHA

     (reads ad)
"White pretty man seeks you and me with brains."

MARY

That's not the one.

SAMANTHA

I got it now. I got it.
     (reads ad)
"Affectionate, warm, well-bred stud enjoys sleazy
thin women."
     (to Mary)
Damn, I want him!

(Samantha points to tear in paper.)

SAMANTHA

     (continuing)
I can't see the phone number.

MARY

Don't you blame me, you bitch. You're the one that
wanted to hog the whole paper to yourself.

> (Samantha in a rage, knocks over
> chairs. They both flip tables and
> coffee table, pull on each other's
> clothing.)

                    MARY
     (continuing)
Get your filthy hands off of me. You bitch.

                    SAMANTHA
Well, if you weren't so damn desperate we could have
landed our husbands tonight, but nooo, you had to
rip the paper.

> (Samantha crumples and tears paper,
> stomps with foot. Mary kneels, sadly
> stares at paper, crushes it to her
> chest.)

                    MARY
It was my only hope.

> (Samantha kneels, sits on floor. Puts
> cigarette in Mary's mouth.)

                    SAMANTHA
All you need is a smoke, c'mon now. Take a deep
breath. There you go.

> (Mary inhales, rolls on floor with
> drink in hand, cigarette in lips
> broken.)

                    MARY
I don't want a smoke.
     (screams)
I need a husband!

                    SAMANTHA
Damn men.

                    MARY
Bloody damn men.

> (Samantha's arm on Mary's shoulder.
> Mary's eyes widen.)

                    SAMANTHA
After all we've been through together and this is
our fate. Just you and me and the world.

> (Mary recoils. Samantha wipes Mary's
> hair. Mary's eyes expand wider.)

                    MARY
Yeah, after all we've been through together and
we're still alone.

                        SAMANTHA
Yep, just you and me, me and you, darling. Maybe it
was meant to be this way?

                        (Mary guzzles drink.)

                        MARY
I'm not happy.

                        SAMANTHA
Yes you are, darling. You're gay as the singing
sparrow in spring, soaring over--

                        MARY
The damn Tomcats below.

                        SAMANTHA
Searching for the one you truly love.

                        (Mary stares at Samantha.)

                        MARY
You've always been here for me, Sam.

                        (Samantha moves closer, gently wipes
                        tear from Mary's cheek.)

                        SAMANTHA
And I always will, honey. Always. I promise.

                        (They both lock eyes. Samantha's
                        confused, backs away a bit.)

                        SAMANTHA
     (continuing)
What? What? Why are you looking at me like that?

                        (Romance in Mary's expression.)

                        MARY
I thought, I felt, I wanted you to kiss me. You
know?

                        (Samantha recoils, frowns.)

                        SAMANTHA
Kiss you? On the lips?

                        MARY
Sort of, like in the movies.

                        (Mary extends her tongue. Samantha
                        rolls on floor with her drink.)

                        MARY
     (continuing)
What? What's wrong?

                              SAMANTHA
You're drunk with ecstasy. I may be fat, but this
is no beer belly, darling.

                                   (Mary and Samantha rise to wavering
                                   feet, stare, but keep distance.)

                              MARY
I thought you loved me.

                                   (Samantha frowns, smiles, frowns, face
                                   distorts.)

                              SAMANTHA
      (stuttering)
I, do love you, sort of.

                              MARY
Then marry me!

                              SAMANTHA
Oh, my God! If you are in heaven come to me now and
get me out of here.

                                   (Mary staggers drunk, lips puckered.)

                              SAMANTHA
      (continuing)
Stay away from me, you foul woman. I'm not your man.

                              MARY
But your name is, Sam.

                                   (Samantha stomps foot to floor BOOM!
                                   Thunder. Lights flicker.)

                              SAMANTHA
Now look what you've done.

                                   (Lights out, then slowly brighten.)

                              GOD (V.O.)
      (prolonged deep woman's voice)
Sam. Sam. Where art thou?

                                   (A woman appears in jogging outfit,
                                   smokes cigarette.)

                              MARY
Who are you?

                                   (Samantha gasps.)

                              SAMANTHA
It's God.

                                   (Samantha hides behind Mary.)

                          SAMANTHA
     (continuing)
Tell her I'm not here.

                            GOD
Come to me my darlings.

                          SAMANTHA
     (to Mary)
This shouldn't be happening. There's bad liqueur in
this place.
     (to God)
I don't want to die. I'm not ready for heaven.

                    (God frowns.)

                            GOD
Heaven?
     (laughs)
You will go to hell for your miserable failures.

                           MARY
Take me now, God. Life here is not worth living
without a husband.

                         (Samantha tries to run. God blocks her
                         path, grabs her by the arm.)

                          SAMANTHA
Let go of me. Ow! You're hurting me.

                            GOD
Git over here.

                    (Drags Samantha to F.)

                           MARY
Leave her alone, you, you, brute.

                         (God grabs Mary by the collar, drags
                         her to F.)

                            GOD
Now you both listen to me. I put you two on earth
for a purpose, my purpose.

                    (Samantha falls to knees.)

                          SAMANTHA
Oh, please, tell me my purpose in this forsaken life.

                    (God is disgusted, eyes roll up.)

                            GOD
     (to Samantha)
Look at you. You're makeup is wrong, your blush is
out of balance. Must I do everything for you?

SAMANTHA

That's what God is for. To help us in our time of
need.
     (yells)
I want to be thin!

GOD

Oh, no. No way, babe. Last time I made thin women
they sinned, and sinned, and sinned. Even the Devil
complained Hell was overpopulated. Never again!

SAMANTHA

Look at me. I prayed for a bombshell figure and my
butt exploded.

                         (Samantha's hands expand by hips.)

SAMANTHA
     (continuing)
I promise. I won't abuse my sexy, voluptuous, body.

GOD

I made you perfect and it was a mistake. I had to
take extreme corrective action to save your soul.

SAMANTHA

But men don't marry souls, they marry, luscious,
sensualistic bodies. Something, I don't have. I
want my figure back!

                         (God stares angrily.)

SAMANTHA
     (continuing)
My butt is so much larger than my head I look like,
like... an insect.

                         (Samantha pouts. God drags on
                          cigarette.)

MARY

What about me?

SAMANTHA
     (to God)
Don't mind her. She didn't call you. I paid for
this visit, not her.

                         (God zips finger along lips.)

MARY

Isn't anyone going to speak to me? I must have a
purpose?

                           SAMANTHA
Shut-up!
     (to God)
She's a lesbian. Tried to come on to me, that's
when I called you.

                             GOD
Tsk. Even I have a difficult time trying to figure
you both out.

                                  (God reaches for a drink, guzzles it,
                                  wipes mouth with arm.)

                           MARY
I demand a husband. A storybook wedding.

                           SAMANTHA
Don't you speak in such tones to our heavenly lady.

                             GOD
I like a woman with spunk.

                                  (God blows smoke in Samantha's face.)

                           MARY
I was born to be married. It's my right to snag a
man and keep him by my side forever, and ever, and
ever, 'till nothing of him remains but dust.

                             GOD
A wonderful prayer, Mary.

                                  (Samantha's stunned.)

                           SAMANTHA
I demand a husband.

             GOD   MARY
          Shut-up!   Shut-up!

                                  (Samantha's lips purse, pouts. God
                                  wraps arm around Mary, they chit-chat
                                  as they step to bar, pour drinks.)

                             GOD
You should see what the Angels are wearing now,
Mary. Absolutely glorious, incredibly stunning.

                           SAMANTHA
What about me?
                                  (Samantha's hand to chin, thinking.)

                           SAMANTHA
     (continuing; sorrowfully)
I have needs too.
     (yells)
I want a husband!

(God and Mary turn and stare.)

                              MARY
How dare you raise your voice to God? Get on your
knees and beg her forgiveness.

                              (Samantha stands defiant, hands on
                              hips.)

                              MARY
     (continuing)
Kneel! Kneel! Or the plagues of cellulite shall
come forth upon you.

                              SAMANTHA
I'm already afflicted with that. I have locust in
my garden, frogs in my birdbath, fire in my eyes,
ice in my mind, and my thighs scream at me to stop
eating cookies. What more could I possibly endure?

                              GOD
Oh, stop it, both of you. We are women. We are to
behave like women.
     (to Samantha)
I forgive you of your sins.

                              SAMANTHA
What sins?
     (yells)
I have no damn man to sin with!

                              MARY
Liar! She came on to me. She's the lesbian.

                              (God laughs.)

          SAMANTHA   MARY
     What's so funny?   What's so funny?

                              (God lights another cigarette.)

                              GOD
You're not lesbians, your lonely women and I know
just the cure.

                              (Samantha and Mary leap with joy.)

                              SAMANTHA
A husband at last.

                              MARY
Oh, thank God!

                              GOD
Whoa, not so hasty, ladies. I can perform miracles
but in some cases, well--

```
         SAMANTHA                        MARY
       Well?                         Well, what?
```

                                  (God rubs chin, thinks hard.)

                    GOD
Lets go shopping.

                                  (They leap and hug, exit R. with God's
                                  arms wrapped around their shoulders.)

                    GOD
     (continuing)
I know this wonderful place with all the latest
fashions, I'm talking hot stuff men simply can't
resist. You should see the powder room I have in
heaven... it's absolutely gorgeous.

                                  (Delbert and Simon enter L. See place
                                  is a wreck.)

                    DELBERT
They were here all right.

                                  (Simon sniffs the air.)

                    SIMON
I can smell their odor. Wine and perfume. We
missed them again, Delbert.

                    DELBERT
For some strange reason they are living in this
joint and the doors are always unlocked. I don't
get it. I just don't catch the scene here.

                                  (They pour beers.)

                    DELBERT
     (continuing)
Well two can play the game.

                    SIMON
Oh, no. No way. We were drunk.

                    DELBERT
Shut up. We're gonna do it.

                    SIMON
I don't know. They obviously don't like us, Simon.
They are very beautiful... rude and abusive witches.

                                  (Simon rubs chin, thinks, then smiles.
                                  Delbert and Simon high-five. Guzzle a
                                  huge amount of beer. They laugh, kick
                                  feet like children.)

                            SIMON
          (continuing; serious.)
Delbert, what do you see when you look into a
woman's eyes?

                            DELBERT
I see the future.

                            SIMON
What sort of future? A good one?

                            DELBERT
I see her telling me to take out the trash, wash the
car, cut the grass, paint the fence, and stop having
fun.

                         (Simon's depressed.)

                            DELBERT
          (continuing)
Oh, cheer up ol'chap. What do you see when you gaze
into a woman's eyes?

                            SIMON
Sex.

                            DELBERT
You fool! That's what they want you to see. It's
all an illusion, Simon. That's why all married men
are miserable trouts. They were promised abundant
sex and get next to nothing but bills and a nagging
bitch screaming at them. Honey, do this. Honey, do
that. I wasn't born to be a honey-do! Men have a
higher purpose in life.

                            SIMON
I can't help it, Delbert. I see naughty things in
their eyes and it makes my--

                            DELBERT
I don't want to hear it.

                            SIMON
It makes my thing big and --

                            DELBERT
I said, I don't want to hear it!

                            SIMON
When are you going to get married?

                         (Delbert gags on drink.)

                            DELBERT
Don't you mention that four-letter word with an
I.E.D. attached to it. You know how it upsets me?

                    SIMON
Perhaps therapy would--

                    DELBERT
Never going back to that nutcracker psychiatrist.
He tried to turn me into a homosexual.

                    SIMON
You too?

                         (They both gaze for a beat.)

                    SIMON
     (continuing)
You're not... are you?

                         (Delbert guzzles drink. They reset
                         couch and sit down.)

                    DELBERT
Let's talk about something else.

                    SIMON
It's important to know, Delbert.

                    DELBERT
Just because I love to be a bachelor doesn't make me
gay. Are you gay?
                    SIMON
I was once... I mean happy, you know?

                    DELBERT
No, I don't know. Answer my question. Are you or
not one hell of a happy gay blade?

                    SIMON
If I told you the truth, would you respect me in the
morning?
                         (Delbert sets drink on coffee table,
                         rises, shocked. Simon rises. Both
                         waver on feet, drunk.)

                    SIMON
     (continuing)
Well, what the hell do you want me to say, huh? Oh,
yes dear, I'm gay and I love you very much, Delbert.

                         (Delbert steps back, fist clenched.
                         Simon presses on.)

                    DELBERT
Get away from me, Simon. I'm warning you.

                    SIMON
I've always loved you, Delbert. Come into my arms.
Look into my eyes. What do you see?

                                    DELBERT
I see a black eye.

                              (Delbert swings fist. Simon ducks.
                              Delbert falls down, Simon leaps on him.)

                                    SIMON
                    (Lips puckered, kissing sounds)
          Come to me, Delbert. Wrap your big strong arms
          around--

                                    DELBERT
Your bloody neck.

                              (They choke each other. Both run out of
                              air, break up, roll on floor.)

                                    DELBERT
                    (continuing)
          Stay away from me, you, you, perverted --

                                    SIMON
Reflection of yourself.

                              (Delbert stares as Simon rises and
                              steps to bar.)

                                    SIMON
                    (continuing)
          That's what's going to happen to us if we don't get
          married. The loneliness will compel us to bond
          together just like that shrink said would happen.

                              (Delbert rises, approaches bar.)

                                    DELBERT
Oh, no. That's not going to happen.

                                    SIMON
So now you're ready to talk about marriage?

                                    DELBERT
Not with you.

                                    SIMON
Of course not with me, stupid. With Samantha and
Mary.

                              (Delbert paces, hand to chin.)

                                    DELBERT
You really think? You know?

                                    SIMON
The doctor said so. At times I've had the urge to
hug you.

(Delbert cocks his fist.)

DELBERT

You sonofabitch. Stay away from me. I mean it.

SIMON

Only when I'm drunk.

DELBERT

You need to quit drinking. And you don't need a
woman. I don't need a woman.

(Simon stares with hope, leaps on
Delbert.)

SIMON

Darling! You've come home.

(Simon passes out.)

DELBERT

That does it. No more drinking for you. And no
more psychiatrists too!

(Delbert drags Simon out to R. exit.
Delbert returns, lights cigarette,
grabs drink.)

DELBERT
    (continuing; to himself)
Maybe it's for the best. Samantha does have the
machinery a man could enjoy. So what if I have to
take out the trash and paint the fence?

(Delbert guzzles drink, exits drunk.)

(Delbert and Simon both fearfully
backup onto stage. SFX. BOOM!)

(A red Devil enters, pointed tail,
pitchfork in hand. Spooky music in
b.g. Red lights wash stage.)

DEVIL
    (polite)
Hello, Simon. Hello, Delbert.

(Devil takes cigarette from Delbert,
tosses it to floor.)

DEVIL
    (continuing)
You shouldn't smoke. It's bad for your wellbeing.
You know how much I care about you boys.

                              SIMON
You! You're really the devil?
      (points to Delbert)
He made me do it.

                              (Delbert slaps Simon's finger.)

                              DEVIL
Stop it. I abhor violence. Listen to me, boys.
I've come to inform you that there are unseen powers
to be that are keeping you single. When I created
you I never meant for you boys to be lonely and
drunk.

                              DELBERT
You created us? Oh, no. No way.

                                   (Devil wraps arm around Delbert.
                                    Delbert flinches in pain, breaks away.)

                              DEVIL
Oh, I'm sorry. Residual heat. The weather is
always a bit warm in Hell.

                              DELBERT
Get away. Begone, Satan. Leave this holy place.

                                   (Devil laughs.)

                              DEVIL
Tsk. Tsk. Tsk. Delbert, Delbert, Delbert. How vain
of you to believe all those lies people say about
me. I'm your friend.

                              SIMON
Like a guardian angel?

                              DEVIL
Exactly.

                              DELBERT
I'm not interested. Go away.

                                   (Delbert runs. Devil points finger.
                                    SFX. BOOM! Lights flicker. Delbert's
                                    feet glued to floor.)

                                   (Simon dives behind a table.)

                              DEVIL
You listen to me, you little... child of my beloved
grace. Samantha is the girl of your dreams. I made
girls like her just for boys like you. She's a
wonder girl and she'll make your life very, very,
interesting and exiting.

                              DELBERT
What sort of excitement you have in mind?

                        DEVIL
Well, I hate to say that word, you know?

                        SIMON
Sex?

                        (Devil shyly shrugs shoulders, nods.)

                        DEVIL
I wish there was another word for it, it just sounds
so uncouth.

                        SIMON
Mr. Devil, I'm ready to make a deal.

                        DEVIL
A deal?

                        (Devil snaps fingers. Delbert's feet
                        are free.)

                        DELBERT
Don't sell your soul to him, Simon. Don't do it.

                        DEVIL
Ta-ta, tsk, oh. We don't do those things. I'm not
here to force you boys into doing anything you don't
want to do.

                        DELBERT
You're not?

                        DEVIL
Of course not. If you don't want to marry, Samantha.
     (to Simon)
And you don't want eternal love from, Mary.
     (to Delbert)
Just say so and your will be done. No problem.
I'll leave and... you both can have each other for
the rest of your miserable lives.

                        (Devil waves his cape around Delbert
                        and Simon.)

                        (Delbert's arms struggle, but to no
                        avail hugs Simon. His lips pucker to
                        kiss Simon.)

                        DEVIL
     (continuing)
Go on, Delbert. Kiss the man of your dreams.

                        (Devil eerily laughs, jabs pitchforks at
                        them. Waves cape in a strong manner,
                        clawed hand extended. Delbert almost
                        kisses Simon. Simon screams.)

                              (Spell is broken. Delbert kicks Devil
                              in the butt.)

                         DELBERT

Be gone!

                         SIMON

Don't listen to him, stay, please.

                         DELBERT

Don't listen to him, Simon. He's the father of
lies.

                         DEVIL

I'm sorry. I can't stay where I'm not welcome. I
will pray for you, Simon, and you, Delbert. My
blessing I give you. Do the right thing. Take the
ladies as your wives. For great things behold those
who take what they deserve.

                              (Lights flicker, thunder BOOMS! Red
                              lights out, Devil is gone. White
                              lights on.)

                         SIMON

Now look what you've done. You ruined everything.

                         DELBERT

You tell anyone what happened here, I'll kill you.

                              (Delbert violently grabs Simon's arm,
                              drags him to R. exit.)

                         SIMON

I promise I won't tell, Delbert. I can keep a
secret. Like the time we went to that secretarial
Christmas party and you strung mistletoe on your
zipper? I never told your mother about that.

     CURTAIN FALLS.

     (END OF SCENE C)

SCENE D

     BAR IS EMPTY - FURNITURE REASSEMBLED.

     AT RISE:
                              (Samantha and Mary enter from R.
                              wearing bicycle pants, low-cut see-
                              through blouses, high heels, fancy
                              hats.)

                         MARY

This is all your fault. I'd be married by now if
your little gimmicks didn't backfire.

                        SAMANTHA
My fault? I can't help it if your too old and no
man wants you.

                        (Mary's sad.)

                        SAMANTHA
    (continuing)
I'm sorry. I didn't mean to say that, even though
it is true.

                        MARY
What are we going to do? I'm desperate.

                        SAMANTHA
We can pray.

                        MARY
Pray? To who? Cleopatra? God said she's too busy
to help out.

                        (Samantha nods. Mary smirks. Samantha
                        on one knee.)

                        SAMANTHA
    (prays)
Oh, darling of the ages. Beholder of charm,
elegance, glamour and desire. Come forth to show us
the way so Mary can believe... she has no faith in
thee.

                        MARY
Oh, cut out the nonsense.

                        (Chimebells ring, lights flicker, blue
                        lights flood stage. Mary recoils,
                        screams. Cleopatra arrives from ladies
                        room.)

                        CLEOPATRA
You again? What do you want from me now?

                        SAMANTHA
    (to Mary)
Oh-ma-gosh. This isn't supposed to be happening.

                        MARY
Tell her to go away.

                        SAMANTHA
    (to Cleopatra)
We need men for marriage.

                        CLEOPATRA
I told you I've been that route. It doesn't work.
Why must you persist?

MARY
Is it really you? Cleopatra?

CLEOPATRA
No, I'm Ceasar's ghost in drag.

SAMANTHA
Don't piss her off, Mary. She packs a snake.

(Samantha stabs fingers like fangs.)

MARY
What is the secret to beauty? Tell us.

CLEOPATRA
Lots of makeup, expensive eyeliner, fine nylons,
tight clothes and big breasts. Especially the
breasts. In my day we padded our bras with palm fur.
     (scolding)
Today, you women have every conceivable synthetic
contraption and you still can't latch a decent man.
Incompetence, I hate incompetence.

MARY
You bitch! We didn't ask you for your opinion.

SAMANTHA
She didn't mean that.

(Cleopatra stares eye-to-eye with Mary.)

CLEOPATRA
Listen, you little tramp. I've had more men than
you'll ever have, real men, Kings, Pharos, Ceasars --

SAMANTHA
Stop it! Stop! We don't want a fight, we want
advice.

CLEOPATRA
     (to Samantha)
My advice is to get rid of the ballast, my love.

SAMANTHA
I've tried. I'm addicted to chocolate and sweet
things.

(Cleopatra points to Mary.)

CLEOPATRA
Did you see that ballast? She's a failure as a
woman. She'll drag you down into the pit of
damnation. She's a descendant of a Phoenician slave
girl.
     (to Mary)
I knew your ancient relatives. Bad blood. Worked
in the royal latrines.

                          MARY
How dare you!

                                    (Mary slaps Cleopatra. They all scream
                                    as Mary and Cleopatra slapfight.
                                    Samantha vibrates with anxiety, steps
                                    between, breaks them up.)

                          SAMANTHA
     (stutters)
Bub! Bub! Bub! Bub! Uh! Sh..tict, stop!
     (beat)
Ub-ah! Ub-ah! Ub-ah!

                                    (Samantha vibrates, swings hands
                                    downward, foot stomps floor.)

                          SAMANTHA
     (continuing)
Stop!

                          MARY
     (to Cleopatra)
She started it.

                          CLEOPATRA
She deserved it.

                                    (They both arch their backs like cats,
                                    hiss at each other.)

                          SAMANTHA
Bah-uh! Bah-uh!

                                    (Samantha's in the middle of all this,
                                    points to each and herself, childlike.)

                          MARY
Just tell that rich bitch to stay away from me.

                          CLEOPATRA
Jealous.

                          MARY
You're dead! I'm alive.

                                    (Cleopatra's stunned.)

                          SAMANTHA
     (to Mary)
Don't, don't. Shush-up.

                                    (Mary struts proudly around Cleopatra.)

MARY
          (to Cleopatra)
Yeah, you had your fine days. Well now it's my turn
to live, bitch Queen from hell. Look at yourself.
Fabulous you were. Not anymore. You're dead! Go
back to the grave where you belong. I don't need
you to get a man.

                         (Cleopatra bows head, slowly leaves.)

SAMANTHA
She doesn't mean it. Don't go, please.
          (to Mary)
Now look what you've done.

                         (Mary points with authority.)

MARY
          (to Cleopatra)
Go back into your tomb, you gorgeous witch. How
dare you flaunt your fabulous body in my presence.
And don't come back to torture us living souls.

SAMANTHA
          (screams to Mary)
Shut-up!

                         (Samantha dives to floor, grabs
                         Cleopatra's foot as she slowly walks
                         away.)

SAMANTHA
          (continuing)
Ahhhgh! Don't leave me in this world.

CLEOPATRA
You cannot enter the underworld unmarried. The
ridicule is relentless and unmerciful. It's hell,
my dear. Find a sucker, I mean, a man, then you
come see me. I have a fantastic hot wax tub that's
just out of this world.

                         (Lights dim, Cleopatra exits. Samantha
                         sobs on the floor. Mary comforts her.
                         Samantha rises, steps to F.)

SAMANTHA
You had no right to insult her. She's a Queen.

MARY
Some Queen. Did you see her angles? Sits on her
royal throne basking day and night buttering up her
face like a streetwalker. She's fat!

                         (Mary slaps her butt.)

SAMANTHA
You would be too if you had to lie in a some unknown
sarcophagus six-thousand years with no one to talk
to.

MARY
She's not your friend, Sam. I am.

SAMANTHA
Little comfort coming from a slave girl.

MARY
That bitch is lying. Lying just to make herself
look better than me. I would never do anything like
that, Sam.

(Samantha frowns.)

MARY
(continuing)
I don't like this praying stuff at all. We are
women and all women know how to snag men. We don't
need extraterrestrial assistance.

SAMANTHA
Okay, but she's right about one thing. We do need
larger breasts. Huge pendulous breasts that sway
like palm trees in a summer breeze.

MARY
We do not. They are big enough as is.

`CURTAIN FALLS.

(END OF SCENE D)

ACT III

SCENE E

AT RISE:

(Samantha and Mary enter from R.)

MARY
Oh, gawsh, Sam. It's... it's day three. I got to
get married today!

(R. Door jiggles. They run into ladies
room.)

(Bartender, Delbert and Simon enter.
A crowd of patrons also enter take
seats. Discjockey plays music.)

                              (Delbert and Simon take drinks, stand
                              F. Samantha and Mary poke heads from
                              door, listening.)

                    DELBERT
Simon, I've been thinking about getting married.

                    SIMON
You have? You?

                              (Delbert nods.)

                    SIMON
          (continuing)
Well you can, but not me. Every time I look into a
woman's eyes I hear wedding bells and the clang of
trash cans ringing in my ears.

                              (Delbert pokes pinky into ear,
                              twisting, shakes head, then holds his
                              chin in deep thought.)

                    SIMON
          (continuing)
Snap out of it, Delbert. You don't want a wife.
What you need is a mother. Someone to pamper you,
feed you, scold you, and put you to bed.
          (second thoughts)
That's what wives do, huh?

                              (Delbert nods.)

                    DELBERT
Not to change the subject, but when are we going to
get back to work?

                    SIMON
I spoke with Alex in jail. Said he's working out a
deal.

                    DELBERT
Alex? I don't want to work with that slumbum
producer. He takes advantage of women.

                    SIMON
You were the one that said women should be used as
meat. You eat them and--

                    DELBERT
Shut-up!

                              (Delbert nervously looks over shoulder.)

                    DELBERT
          (continuing)
This place is infested with women. Now just shut up.

                                    (Simon sips his drink. Delbert takes
                                    it.)

                          SIMON
Hey?

                          DELBERT
No more drinking for you. You came on to me again.

                          SIMON
I did not. It's you, you're the one that's a
frustrated old man seeking out perverted fantasies
at my expense. Give me back my drink.

                                    (They fight for the drink, spill both
                                    of them. Women leave their seats with
                                    napkins wiping up the mess. Give them
                                    dirty looks.)

                          FIRST WOMAN
Bunch of slobs.

                          SECOND WOMAN
Clean up your own mess.

                                    (Delbert and Simon stare at their
                                    wiggling bodies.)

                          DELBERT
See? I told you they are perfect slaves.

                                    (Women overhear, grab pocket books, and
                                    pelt them out the door.)

                          FIRST WOMAN
If I see you pigs in here again I'll personally
thrust my high heel up your butt.

                          SECOND WOMAN
Get out and stay out.

                                    (Woman go back to their seats.)

                                    (Samantha and Mary enter in mini-
                                    skirts. Huge breasts expand from
                                    blouses. Men stare as they sit on R.
                                    couch.)

                          SAMANTHA
See? Their buggery eyeballs almost fell out.

                                    (Mary takes a deep breath expanding her
                                    breasts. Wicked Pete falls off stool.)

                          MARY
I hate men who wear high heels.

SAMANTHA
Cowboy boots, Mary.

MARY
Where's Simon and Garfunkle?

(Both laugh. Breasts jiggle.)

SAMANTHA
Probably chasing down some flat-chested broads.

MARY
What if this doesn't work?

SAMANTHA
It will, trust me. Cleopatra knows her stuff.

(Mary fixes her left breast.)

MARY
This one is low on air. I told you to pump it up
more.

(Samantha removes pressure gage from
purse. Mary inserts it down blouse
Pssst!)

MARY
     (continuing)
It's five pounds off.

SAMANTHA
Forget it. It's too late now.

(Delbert and Simon enter in fine suits,
diamond rings on fingers, wear dark
shades and white hats.)

MARY
Well get a load of this, Simon and Garfunkle arrived.

SAMANTHA
Wiggle the bait, darling.

(They rise, wiggle as they walk to
restroom past Delbert and Simon.)

(Delbert and Simon's eyes expand.)

SIMON
Look at those jellybeans.

DELBERT
Shhhh! Those nasty women are still here. Play it
cool, man.

(They sit on couch. Waitress brings
them beers.

                              Simon tips waitress with a quarter.
                              She looks at them, throws the quarter
                              at Delbert's chest.)

                         WAITRESS
Big spenders.

                         SIMON
High-rollers from Vegas, honey.

                              (All the women hear, turn heads, smile.
                              Waitress leaves.)

                         DELBERT
All women think of is money, money, money. They are
so materialistic.

                         SIMON
Yeah, whatever happened to the good ol' days when
women loved a man for being a man? Can't they get
it into their thick skulls they were made to be
barefoot and pregnant?

                              (A shower of water from the ladies
                              drinks drench them.)

                         DELBERT
Only kidding, ladies.

                              (Ladies stare scornfully.)

                         DELBERT
    (continuing)
Drinks on the house.
    (to Bartender)
Put it on my tab.

                              (Ladies giggle.)

                         SIMON
You don't have a tab?

                         DELBERT
They won't know.

                              (Bartender arrives with hand out.
                              Delbert frowns, hands bills over.)

                         SIMON
That's our rent money!

                         BARTENDER
Ask me if my bleeding heart cares?

                         DELBERT
Don't you know who we are? It's us, Delbert and
Simon.

                              (Bartender looks closely. Gasps.)

                         BARTENDER
Oh, I'm so sorry, sir. Here, take your money.

                              (Hands money back, kisses their rings.
                              Backs away to bar.)

                         SIMON
What the hell was that all about?

                         DELBERT
I don't know, but it's got something to do with them.

                              (Delbert points as Samantha and Mary
                              exit restroom and approach.)

                         DELBERT
     (continuing)
I swear they are up to a big dirty trick, but I
can't figure it out.

                         SIMON
They could be connected with the mob.

                              (Delbert frowns.)

                         SAMANTHA
Well, look what we have here.

                         MARY
Two little boys in search of a sandbox to play in?

                              (They wiggle their breasts. Delbert
                              and Simon's eyes expand.)

                         SAMANTHA
Well, aren't you going to invite us to join you?

                              (Before they can answer, Samantha and
                              Mary leap on their laps.)

                         SIMON
Gosh, you're as light as air, Mary.

                         DELBERT
Hello, Sam.

                              (Samantha and Mary peck them on the
                              cheek and giggle, wiggling their
                              breasts.)

                              (Delbert rises, Samantha falls to
                              floor.)

                         DELBERT
     (continuing)
I demand you tell us what is going on here?

(Samantha and Mary both fold lips.)

                    SAMANTHA   MARY
              Nothing, honey.   Nothing, honey.

                              DELBERT
Nothing, honey? You both are rehearsing something
and I want to know our part in this charade.

                              (Samantha rises from floor, brushes
                              herself off.)

                              SAMANTHA
Oh, darling. Don't you like our attire?

                              (They wiggle their breasts. Delbert
                              grabs Samantha.)

                              DELBERT
Enough! Now you listen to me. I don't want to get
married, I don't want a wife, I don't want to take
out the trash. You understand the meaning of this?

                              (Delbert storms off. Samantha tackles
                              him to floor. Her breasts sway over
                              his eyes. Music stops, crowd stares.)

                              SAMANTHA
I'm not forcing you to do anything.

                              (Breasts sway like hypnotic clocks.)

                              DELBERT
Stop it. You're hurting me.

                              (Mary pushes Simon down on couch, does
                              the same.)

                              SIMON
Ow! Ow! Ouch!

                              SAMANTHA
Gaze into my eyes my dear Delbert.

                              (He can't. Breasts obstruct view.)

                              SAMANTHA
                    (continuing; screams)
I said look into my eyes.

                              DELBERT
I can't.

                              (POW! A boob explodes. Samantha
                              rises, storms to ladies room. Pokes
                              head out, whistles. Mary follows.)

                          DELBERT
       (continuing)
Did you hear an explosion?

                              (Simon wags head, rubs forehead.)

                          SIMON
My head is busting. They got huge boobs, Delbert.
My brain gets fuzzy when I see them.

                          DELBERT
They didn't before.

                          SIMON
Maybe they had them special bras that packs 'em in
like sardines. Some women don't like big breasts.

                          DELBERT
That's a lie. They just say that, but they still
wear bras to make 'em stick into your eyes.

                          SIMON
Yeah, you're right, Delbert. No bones about it. I
checked and found that only female mosquitoes bite,
just like you said.

                              (Delbert grabs chin.)

                          SIMON
       (continuing)
What's wrong?

                          DELBERT
I'm confused.
                              (Simon sits on couch. Delbert wanders.
                              Samantha and Mary exit ladies room
                              wearing hippie bell-bottom pants,
                              paisley blouse, platform shoes.)

                              (Mary orders drink at bar, flirting
                              with men. Samantha sits by Simon.)

                          SAMANTHA
Simon? Mary is special, isn't she?

                          SIMON
Oh, yes. She's gorgeous. A wonderful woman these
sad eyes behold, but I can't understand her.

                              (Samantha touches Simon's cheek.)

                          SAMANTHA
Now, now. Don't be so critical. She's a frail
woman. Mary wants to be your mother.

                          SIMON
Huh? Mother?

SAMANTHA
She doesn't believe in marriage in the traditional
sense, nag, bitch, manipulate, or lie.

SIMON
What? Delbert say's all women --

SAMANTHA
Shush my love. Don't you listen to that man. You
need to do what your heart tells you to do. Obey
your inner desires.

                    (Simon sees Mary's body sway.)

SAMANTHA
     (continuing)
You like that, Simon?

SIMON
Yes. I do.

SAMANTHA
See? Those words were not as hard as you thought
they were to say. Say it again, Simon.

                    (Samantha slowly waves finger back and
                    forth past Simon's eyes.)

SIMON
I do. I do. I do.

SAMANTHA
What do you feel, Simon?

SIMON
I feel sleazy. I feel weakened like my brain
doesn't function, and my toy is --

                    (Samantha covers his mouth.)

SAMANTHA
Shut up. You don't have to say it. We know it's
arousing you.

SAMANTHA
     (continuing; yells)
Oh, Mary.
                         (Mary turns, smiles, arrives, sits on
                         Simon's lap. Simon smiles.)

SAMANTHA
     (continuing)
What a perfect couple. I just love him.

                         (Samantha affectionately messes up
                         Simon's hair. As Samantha turns to
                         walk away, Delbert stands over her.)

                              DELBERT
What is going on here?   Simon, you okay?

                              (Simon in a daze.)

                              MARY
Mind your own business.

                              SAMANTHA
Just a little social talk.

                              DELBERT
What did you do to him?

                              SAMANTHA
     (aghast)
How dare you insinuate our moral character. Just
because you're frigid and womanless you have no
authority to question our integrity.

                              DELBERT
Your conscience is overflowing onto the floor.

                              (Samantha searches the floor.)

                              SAMANTHA
It is not.

                              (Soft song plays.)

                              MARY
     (screams)
She doesn't have a conscience.

                              SAMANTHA
Shut-up!
     (to Delbert)
Oh, I love that song.

                              (Samantha sexily sways her body.
                              Delbert mesmerized.)

                              SAMANTHA
     (continuing)
You understand the meaning of this?

                              (Delbert totally hypnotized.)

                              MARY
     (to Delbert)
Dance with her you fool.
                              (Simon rises.)

                              MARY
     (continuing; to Simon)
Not you. You're staying here with me, forever and
ever. You understand me?

                         (Simon nods.)

                    DELBERT
I'll dance with you, but no tricks. Keep your hands
where I can see them.

                    SAMANTHA
Certainly, Delbert.

                         (They slow dance to F.)

                    SAMANTHA
     (continuing)
They make a wonderful couple don't they?

                              (Delbert sees Mary tearing at Simon's
                              clothes.)

                    DELBERT
Look what she's doing. She's taking advantage of
him in his drunken state.

                    SAMANTHA
Delbert, Delbert, Delbert. He's taking advantage of
her. She's a virgin.

                              (Samantha hugs, cheek-to-cheek.)

                    SAMANTHA
     (continuing)
You can nibble on my ear if you want to.

                              (Samantha wiggles her earrings.
                              Delbert pushes her away a bit.)

                    DELBERT
You can't be trusted. What are you up to, anyway?
It's one antic after another. Strange happenings
repeating themselves like a revolver firing into my
head.

                    SAMANTHA
We are girls, Delbert. Girls.

                              (Samantha's hands drop to Delbert's
                              rear. He lifts her hands upward to
                              hips.)

                    SIMON
Delbert, help! Help!
                              (Mary has Simon pinned down on couch.
                              Delbert breaks dance, pulls Mary off
                              Simon. Delbert sits beside Simon like
                              a protective mother.)

                    DELBERT
It's time for you girls to leave.

                          MARY
Women. We are women.

                          SAMANTHA
That's right, woman.
     (to Bartender)
Bartender? These men are acting mighty strange.

                              (Bartender arrives with beer bottle in
                              hand. Delbert grabs bottle pours it
                              down Samantha's blouse.)

                          SAMANTHA
     (continuing)
You son-of-a-bushwhacker. I'll get you for this.

                              (People at bar laugh. Samantha races
                              to ladies room.)

                          BARTENDER
Hey! This is no gay bar, get out, both of you.

                              (Bartender takes second look.)

                          BARTENDER
     (continuing)
Oh, it's you guys. Ah, you can stay, no problem.
So sorry. Drinks on the house. All you want.

                              (Bartender rushes to bar.)

                          MARY
Get back here! Don't you disobey a woman.

                              (Delbert and Simon rise. Spell wearing
                              off of Simon. Samantha storms out of
                              ladies room, fists clenched.)

                          DELBERT
All right, that's enough. What is going on here?

                          SIMON
I've been raped!

                              (Music stops. Crowd stares. Samantha
                              waves hand to discjockey, music
                              resumes.)

                          DELBERT
Now you listen to me, Samantha --

                          SAMANTHA
No, you listen to me --

                          MARY
And me --

                              SIMON
I've been raped!

                              ALL
Shut-up!

                    (Music stops. Delbert waves hand to
                    discjockey. Music resumes.)

                              SAMANTHA
Look at the scene you have created. You are
embarrassing us.

                    (Samantha and Mary cry, wipe eyes with
                    hanky. Mary snorts into hanky, hands
                    it to Simon.)

                              MARY
     (demanding)
Get me a napkin, now!

                    (Simon obeys. Delbert grabs Simon.)

                              DELBERT
Look into my eyes, Simon. She hypnotized you!

                    (Samantha and Mary cry louder. Two men
                    from bar step up.)

                              FIRST MAN
What's going on here? Can't you manage your
girlfriends?

                              DELBERT
Girlfriends? They ain't our girls.

                              SECOND MAN
Good, we'll comfort them.

                    (Samantha and Mary leap into their
                    arms, crying. They exit.)

                              SIMON
I'm scared, Delbert.

                              DELBERT
Me too. These are weird women and for some strange
reason they got their arrows aimed at us.

                              SIMON
It could be --

                              DELBERT
Shut up. It's not them.

                              SIMON
They said they would get revenge. Remember?

DELBERT
Simon, that was years ago. You were five years old
or so.

SIMON
It still haunts me, Delbert. I didn't like the idea
of playing doctor with them.
     (pokes finger to Delbert's chest)
It was your idea, your sick, perverted, idea.

                    (Delbert sits on couch, hand to cheek,
                    thinking. Simon does same. They look
                    at each other, thinking.)

                    (Samantha and Mary's heads poke from R.
                    entry, watching. Samantha waves hand
                    to discjockey. Music lowers in volume.)

SIMON
     (continuing)
I love her.

DELBERT
     (rapidly)
Don't you say such a thing.

                    (Samantha and Mary smile. With fingers
                    pinched, they tip-toe along bar, hide
                    behind couch.)

SIMON
I can't help it, Delbert. I'm in love with Mary.
I've seen visions of someone like her.

                    (Mary breathes on fingernails, polishes
                    nails to chest.)

DELBERT
Visions? Yeah, you mean nightmares. I had better
plans for you, Simon.

                    (Samantha and Mary frown.)

DELBERT
     (continuing)
I wanted you for myself.
                    (Samantha and Mary's chins sink,
                    exchange a look.)

DELBERT
     (continuing)
Selfish reasons, I suppose.

                    (Delbert and Simon guzzle beer.)

SIMON
I understand, Delbert.

                              (Simon's hand taps Delbert's knee.
                              Delbert slaps it off.)

                         DELBERT
Get your damn hands off of me. What I'm trying to
say is that, we've been a team for a lifetime and
I'm just scared that it's all coming to an end.

                              (Samantha's hand strokes Delbert's
                              hair. Delbert slaps hand.)

                         DELBERT
     (continuing)
Simon, I told you to keep your hands off of me.

                         SIMON
I didn't touch you. Now bug off, bitch.

                              (Samantha lights cigarette, blows smoke
                              past Delbert.)

                         DELBERT
My entire world is going up in smoke.

                              (Simon looks over shoulder. Samantha
                              and Mary duck.)

                         SIMON
You've been like a mother to me, Delbert. Always
looking out for my safety and I appreciate it, you
know?

                              (Samantha's hand squeezes Delbert's
                              ear. Delbert slaps ear.)

                         SIMON
     (continuing)
It wasn't me. It's a fly.

                         DELBERT
I'll stick my shoe up your anus, Simon, if you touch
me again. I mean it.

                              (Delbert and Simon guzzle beer.
                              Waitress replenishes supply. She
                              waddles as she leaves.)

                         DELBERT
     (continuing)
See that, Simon? See how she shakes her bait?
That's exactly what Samantha and Mary are doing to
us. Women have deformed hips, Simon. It's a
evolution leftover from elephants.

                              (Samantha and Mary's heads pop up,
                              extremely upset. High heels in hand
                              poised to bop their heads.)

                          SIMON
They are girls, Delbert. Girls. And I want one.
But now I can't have one because you, you, pissed
them off... and nobody wants to hire us. Our acting
careers are over. Who wants a washed up,
degenerate, unemployed broken man?

                              (Mary attempts to hug Simon. Samantha
                               restrains her, pulls her down.)

                          DELBERT
When did you say Alex was putting a show together?

                              (Simon looks to wall clock.)

                          SIMON
He's out of jail and he's... damn, he's coming here.

                              (Samantha and Mary's heads poke up,
                               surprised. Lip-speak, "Alex?" They
                               crawl away on hands and knees, but
                               forced back as people walk by.)

                          DELBERT
What? Why here? His reputation is sunk here?

                          SIMON
Everywhere. I told him we needed the work.

                          DELBERT
That pervert will destroy our reputations.

                          SIMON
So what? We are already washed up. Nobody wants
old actors.

                              (Mary leaps upward, Samantha pulls her
                               back down by the hair, OW! They
                               slapfight.)

                          SIMON
     (continuing)
Anyway, I signed the contracts.

                          DELBERT
You punk. You forged my name.

                          SIMON
I will lie to a Judge if I must.

                              (Samantha and Mary stop fighting. Cup
                               hands to ear.)

                          DELBERT
Okay. What's the play?

                          SIMON
Sex Kittens In The Litter Box.

                         DELBERT
No way!
                              (Samantha and Mary duck as Delbert
                              looks over his shoulder.)

                         SIMON
So what if you have to get naked before an audience
of six-hundred people, or more. At that distance
it'll look like a peanut floating in a chef's salad.
Look at the bright side, Delbert. You're so
negative.

                         DELBERT
And you?

                         SIMON
I took the policeman's role.

                              (Delbert grabs Simon's collar.)

                         DELBERT
You S.O.B. you got me running around naked!

                         SIMON
You know my hemorrhoids hurt when I run. Now
getting back to reality. What about you and
Samantha? You going to marry the bitch?

                              (Samantha and Mary's heads pop up. Lip-
                              speak, "Bitch?")

                         DELBERT
She's a royal itch isn't she.

                              (Delbert scratches armpit.)

                         DELBERT
    (continuing)
Sort of like a mother hen with no rooster to peck on.

                              (Samantha stares meanly, raises hand to
                              slap Delbert. Mary restrains. Delbert
                              and Simon laugh.)

                         SIMON
Yeah, like lost geese with no goose to goose 'em.

                              (Delbert and Simon explode in laughter.
                              Samantha and Mary not amused.)

                         DELBERT
Inarticulate broads. They think we like 'em. Ha!
Samantha's the sort of woman a man can abuse and get
away with it... and, she's so dumb, she wouldn't
even know it. Ha! She dives into the ocean and
it's high tide, folks! Ha!

SIMON
Ha! I got one for ya. Mary's so skinny and boll-
legged cockroaches offer her a suite in the roach
motel. Ha! And Mary, she's a hot fox with no one
to trot. Ha! She's so lonely her pen pal returns
her letters unopened. Ha! Mary goes for plastic
surgery, the doctor cuts up her credit cards. Ha!
She's so gullible she gets pregnant and says to the
doctor, "Is it mine?"

                         (Delbert and Simon explode in hilarious
                         drunken laughter.)

                         (Samantha and Mary rise to feet, tip
                         couch over, dump Delbert and Simon to
                         floor, then storm into ladies room.
                         Feet pounding hard BOOM! BOOM! BOOM!)

            DELBERT   SIMON
         Earthquake!   Earthquake!

                         (Music stops, patrons stare, approach,
                         grab Delbert and Simon, throw them out.)

                    BARTENDER
       (panic)
It's not me. I'm not doing it. You can stay.

                         (Out they go. Patrons wipe hands and
                         resume activities.)

                         (Samantha and Mary exit ladies room in
                         a rage. Storm about the dance floor,
                         vibrating with panic attacks. Fists
                         pounding their chests.)

                     MARY
I'll kill him. I'll kill him. Sam, like a whisper
on the wind, he's not coming on to me. Could it be
they are monks?

                    SAMANTHA
Yeah, they're monks all right, monkeys!

                     MARY
I'm scared, Sam.

                    SAMANTHA
That does it. They are going to marry us and that's
that. Plan "Z" now in effect. Red alert! Red
alert!
                         (Women at bar turn heads.)

                     WOMEN
       (randomly)
"Shut-up!" "Keep it down!" "Hold your tongue you
belligerent brats."

(Samantha and Mary thumb to nose,
wiggle fingers.)

MARY

A fitting punishment for those mama's boys.

(Bartender resets couch.)

BARTENDER

What happened? Them hitmen will kill me now. I
demand protection.

(Mary hands Bartender a condom.)

SAMANTHA

Don't sweat it, pops. We got everything in control.
We have valuable information from them now.

MARY

But you better go along, 'cause it could go wrong.

(Mary mimics gun to Bartender, pulls
trigger.)

SAMANTHA

Pow! Just like that. Now look, this is what we
want you to do.

(They whisper in his ear.)

BARTENDER

No way!

(They twist his arms, pinch his nose.
Down he goes to his knees.)

(Samantha dangles handcuffs by his
nose.)

BARTENDER
(continuing)
Okay, okay, I said.

(Bartender dashes to bar.)

MARY

Look! It's Delbert's wallet!

SAMANTHA

Give it to me. He's my husband to be. It's my
money.

(They yank it back and forth. Mary
wins.)

(Alex arrives in white suit, dark
shades, gold jewelry. Samantha and
Mary hug him. He resists, to no use.)

                          SAMANTHA
        (continuing)
Darling, Alex.

                          MARY
Ohhh, you little pot roast I could just gobble you
up.

                              (Mary affectionately messes up Alex's
                              hair.)

                          ALEX
What is going on here?

                              (They drag Alex to couch. They sit and
                              fondle him like a cute little boy.)

                          SAMANTHA
        (like a little girl)
We want you to produce a play and we want the
leading roles.

                          ALEX
What kind of play? Hookers on Elm Street?

                          MARY
That's a good one.

                          SAMANTHA
Don't mind her.

                              (Samantha grabs a beer bottle from a
                              passing man's hand, shoves him away.)

                              (Samantha cradles Alex like a newborn
                              babe. Mary slaps a pacifier nipple on
                              bottle. Samantha forces beer down
                              Alex's throat.)

                          SAMANTHA
        (continuing)
That a boy. Drink it all down.

                              (Alex gags, coughs, tries to spit out
                              nipple.)

                          MARY
He could be gay.

                              (Alex sits up coughing. Mary dabs his
                              lips with napkin.)

                          MARY
        (continuing; child-like)
You'll do it for me, darling?

                    SAMANTHA
     (child-like)
And me, honeypie?

                              (Sam rips off nipple from bottle, slams
                              more beer into Alex's mouth.)

                    SAMANTHA
     (continuing)
It's a great plot. Imagine a stage play of gigantic
proportions. Two men, two women, battling the tipsy-
topsy world of --

                    MARY

Shhh!

                              (Mary opens Delbert's wallet, wipes
                              money under Alex's wiggling, sniffing
                              nose.)

                              (Samantha whispers in Alex's ear. Alex
                              nods, snatches the money, smiles.)

          CURTAIN FALLS

          (END OF SCENE E)

                         ACT III

                         SCENE F

          AT RISE:
                              (Alex roams about calling out blocking
                              instructions.)

                              (Samantha and Mary wear high skirts.)

                              (Delbert and Simon enter in blue jeans
                              and cowboy boots, turn to exit when
                              they see Samantha and Mary.)

                    ALEX
Not so fast, buddies. You signed a contract.

                    DELBERT
Yeah, but we didn't agree to work with them ding-
dong broads.
                    ALEX
Hold your tongue. The script's been changed. This
is a respectable show.
                    SIMON
From you? A respectable show? Ha! In ten minutes
everyone will be in underwear pounding thighs on the
floor screaming for mercy.

                                    ALEX
That's all changed. Prison made me into an honest
respectable man... it was a very penetrating
experience. I've rehabilitated. This is the new
me! See?

                                        (Alex spins around like a figure
                                        skater. Grabs a thin script from bar.)

                                    ALEX
        (continuing)
It's titled, "Stage Play." A beautiful romantic
drama.

                                    DELBERT
This I got to see.

                                    SIMON
No, Delbert. I don't feel good about this.
Something bad is gonna happen. I just know it.

                                    DELBERT
We got no money, Simon. I lost the wallet. We got
no rent money.

                                        (Simon panics. Alex wraps arm around
                                        them.)

                                    ALEX
Quit your whimpering. Be professional, boys. It's
only a stage play. And it's going all the way to
Broadway.

                                    DELBERT
What's the motivation?

                                        (Alex hands script to Delbert.)

                                    ALEX
Here's the script.

                                        (Delbert flips pages.)

                                    DELBERT
Plot's thin as ice and corny just like the actresses
who likely wrote it.

                                        (Delbert glances to Samantha. She
                                        looks away.)

                                    DELBERT
        (continuing)
Where's all the pages?

                                    ALEX
We are rehearsing the last of the second and third
act.

                         SIMON
That's odd.

                         ALEX
Look, I don't have time to baby-sit. If you want
the money just do the job. A Broadway theater owner
will be in the pits watching and taping the event.
This one is going big. You in or out? If you're
out, I'll sue you. Blacklist your name, you'll
never work again in this town. Understand the
meaning of this?

                              (Delbert nods. Sees stagehand position
                              video camera on stage.)

                         SIMON
I'm in!
                              (Alex roams about calling directions.)

                         SIMON
     (continuing; to Delbert)
Oh, boy. Broadway, Delbert. We're making it big
this time. Cheer up.

                         DELBERT
It's just that I feel something is not right.

                              (Samantha and Mary hold hands, smile,
                              jumping like little girls at a party.)

                         SIMON
Ahh, it's just left-over feelings, Delbert. Just
pretend you don't know them. Be professional and
treat them just like any other actress. Ya don't
have a choice. It's do or get washed out.

                              (Delbert wags head. Sees Samantha and
                              Mary taking positions at bar.)

                         DELBERT
I don't like it, Simon. But for you, I'll do it.

                         SIMON
For us, Delbert. Do it for us.

                              (Simon hugs Delbert. Delbert pushes
                              him off, raises fist.)

                         DELBERT
Get off of me. I'll slug you.

                         ALEX
Okay, lets go. Act three, page ninety-nine from the
top. Action!

                              (Delbert and Simon approach bar, tap
                              Samantha and Mary on shoulder.)

                            MARY
I thought you'd never ask.

                        (They dance to fast rap music.)

                          SAMANTHA
And you, my dear. Must you dance like a queer?

                          DELBERT
That does it!

                        (Delbert stops dancing, walks away.
                        Music stops.)

                            ALEX
Cut! What's the problem?

                        (Delbert examines script, pounds finger
                        into page.)

                          DELBERT
That line's not in the script and you know it.

                            ALEX
What line?

                          DELBERT
Must you dance like a queer?

                        (Samantha slaps Delbert.)

                          SAMANTHA
How dare you?

                        (Mary slaps Delbert.)

                            MARY
That's disgusting.

                        (Samantha and Mary cry, hug Alex.)

                            ALEX
Okay, children. Listen up. This is a dance scene.
Dialog isn't supposed to be heard.
     (to discjockey)
Turn the music up louder when we go into action.

                        (Delbert stares meanly at Samantha.
                        She stares back. Mary does the same
                        with Simon.)

                            ALEX
     (continuing)
Okay, lets try it again. Music? Action!

                        (Music loud. They dance.)

                    (Samantha and Mary lip-speak. From the
                    expressions on Delbert and Simon's face
                    we can tell they are severe insults.)

                    (They argue at a feverish pitch, but
                    unheard. They push each other in a
                    heated rage.)

                    (Music stops.)

                ALEX
      (continuing)
Great! Fantastic! Okay, we now go to scene "E"
page one-hundred-and-two. from line six. When I say
action, I want passionate action. Got it?

                    (Everyone nods.)

                ALEX
      (continuing)
Action!

                    (Soft music plays.)

                    (Samantha and Mary sit on couch,
                    sipping drinks, rubbing Delbert and
                    Simon's legs.)

                    (After a beat, music stops.)

                ALEX
      (continuing)
Cut!
      (to Delbert)
What's wrong?

              DELBERT
I can't say it.

              SIMON
Damn it, Delbert. It's only a play. That theater
owner is watching and your on video. Stop screwing
up. This is our big chance to break out of poverty.

              DELBERT
Okay, okay. Lets try it again.

                    (Samantha and Mary grin.)

                ALEX
Roll it!

                    (Music resumes.)

              DELBERT
Will you marry me?

> (Samantha leaps on Delbert.)

                    SIMON
Will you marry me?

> (Mary leaps on Simon. They all tumble
> to floor. Music stops.)

                    ALEX
Cut! Superb performance. I love it.

> (Everyone moves to new blocking
> positions.)

> (Samantha and Mary enter ladies room.)

                    SIMON
See, that wasn't so bad was it? If you just
disconnect your emotions from your professional
career.

> (Simon walks stiffly to bar. Delbert
> follows in same manner.)

> (Alex hands them tuxedoes.)

                    ALEX
Now we do the final scene.

                    DELBERT
I don't know, Alex. This is a tough gig.

                    ALEX
     (sympathetic)
Look, I know the situation. It's hard.

                    SIMON
You can say that again.

> (Simon rubs pants. Delbert slaps
> Simon's hand.)

                    ALEX
Look, trust me, okay? It's safe. It's just a stage
play, no more, no less. What's there to be
apprehensive about, huh?

> (Alex wraps arm around them.)

                    DELBERT
It's just that it feels so real.

                    SIMON
Too real.

                        ALEX
And that's the sign of a good script and fine
actors. I'm tellin' ya, boys. This show is gonna
change ya life, forever. It's Broadway, Las Vegas,
Hollywood from here on out.

                              (Alex pinches their cheeks and leaves
                              blocking the actors. Delbert and Simon
                              high-five.)

                        SIMON
Oh, boy, Delbert. It's a dream come true. A real
dream coming true for us. Money, fame, luxury,
women, fine cars.

                        DELBERT
Yeah, I love it already. I can do it, Simon. I'm
motivated. No fear here.

                        SIMON
Right on, partner.

                              (They stick thumbs-up to a man in the
                              audience.)

                        SIMON
      (continuing)
That's the theater owner. He likes us, Delbert.

                              (Delbert and Simon change into
                              tuxedoes. Alex raps on ladies room
                              door.)

                        MARY (V.O.)
We're coming. Hold your tongue.

                              (Alex checks video camera. Snaps
                              fingers, wedding music plays, then
                              stops. Bartender enters as a priest.
                              Delbert and Simon freeze.)

                        ALEX
Loosen up, boys. Relax. It's only a play.

                              (Alex gently slaps Delbert and Simon on
                              cheek. They are jolted awake.)

                              (Samantha flaps arms, squawks like a
                              chicken.)

                        DELBERT
I'm ready, Alex. On with the show!

                              (God enters with cigarette dangling
                              from lips, stares hard at Delbert and
                              Simon.)

                          SIMON
Who's that?

                          DELBERT
Don't know. Sure gives me the chills though.

                    (Cleopatra enters.)

                          SIMON
These people are not in the script. Look at the
outfit she's wearing.

                          DELBERT
Egyptian? I don't get it.
     (yells to Alex)
Alex?

                    (Alex waves arm.)

                          ALEX
Later, I'm too busy. Get ready.

                    (Delbert and Simon take positions by
                    center stage.)

                    (Alex pounds on ladies room door.)

                          ALEX
     (continuing)
You women ready yet? What's taking so long?

                    (Alex faces audience. Mary opens door,
                    burns Alex with cigarette on arm OUCH!)

                    (God grabs Alex by arm. Blows smoke in
                    his face.)

                          GOD
Haven't you men learned anything these past six-
thousand years? Never turn your back on a woman you
silly thing.

                    (Alex backs away.)

                          ALEX
Who are you?

                    (Cleopatra intervenes.)

                          CLEOPATRA
Men, you're all alike. Just do as the lady says and
get on with it.

                          ALEX
I'm the producer here--

                              (God snaps fingers, thunder claps,
                              lights flicker.)

                         ALEX
        (continuing)
... ag, fudge, gumby, doddle-do-wee, ha-ha!

                         GOD
Shall I make yea into a babbling idiot? Send fleas
upon thee?
                              (Cleopatra giggles. Alex vigorously
                              scratches armpits. Delbert and Simon
                              approach.)

                         DELBERT
What is going on here?

                         CLEOPATRA
Dare you raise your voice to women. Look at my feet
when you speak to me!
        (to God)
Strike the arrogant beast with a bolt from above.
Have no compassion on this peasant.

                              (Delbert laughs. God upset. Cleopatra
                              purses lips.)

                         DELBERT
I get it. This is a comedy.
        (to God)
You're Samantha's mother.
        (to Cleopatra)
And you're her father.
                              (Delbert and Simon explode in laughter.
                              God restrains Cleopatra from
                              backhanding them both.)

                         CLEOPATRA
Don't let them speak to you like that, my lady.
They are jealous they are not women.

                              (Delbert and Simon step back to center
                              stage.)

                         GOD
So they want to play tough?

                         CLEOPATRA
Send plagues of pimples so no woman will lay eyes on
them for eternity. Bestow upon them little wee-
wee's to crush their inflated masculine attitudes.
Punish them, my lady. Make them bow to their knees
to worship and glorify us.

                         GOD
No, my child. That's too good for them. I've
already made up my mind.

>   (God drags on her cigarette, blows
>   smoke in Alex's face, itching stops.
>   Samantha and Mary pound on ladies room
>   door.)

                              ALEX
Okay, we're ready. Music, camera on, action!

>   (Wedding music plays. Priest stands at
>   F. Samantha and Mary exit in white
>   wedding gowns, cigarette in lips.)

>   (They shove cigarettes into drinks on
>   bar as they pass.)

                         WHISKEY PETE
          (to Mary)
Last chance, babe. Falling in love could be your
mistake.

>   (Samantha steps on gown, trips, reaches
>   out as she falls pulling Mary down.
>   They both tumble to floor.)

>   (Everyone gasps. Hands cover mouths.)

>   (God's hand rises slowly, lifting
>   Samantha and Mary to their feet.)

                              DELBERT
Simon, I'm scared.

                              SIMON
That's good acting, Delbert.

                              DELBERT
I'm not acting. My knees are shaking.

>   (Delbert's knees vibrate.)

                              SIMON
This seems all too real. My thing is vibrating,
Delbert.
                              DELBERT
Shut up! I don't want to hear it.

>   (Samantha and Mary walk beside Delbert
>   and Simon to priest. Delbert stands
>   left of Priest.)

                              PRIEST
Do you, big man on my left take this sweet lovable
little hummingbird for your wedded wife for life?
     (yells)
Speak up so we all can hear you loud and clear.

>   (Delbert swallows hard. Samantha's
>   foot crushes his toe. OUCH!)

                              DELBERT
I do. I solemnly do.

                              PRIEST
Do you, my foolish man, take this charming butterfly
as your wife till the last breath of your life?

                              SIMON
     (whispers, nervously)
I, I, do.

                              PRIEST
     (yell)
Speak up!

                              SIMON
I, I do.

                                   (God smiles, nods her head. Samantha
                                   and Mary leap up into Delbert's and
                                   Simon's arms. They feel the strain.
                                   They all tumble to floor.)

                              GOD
     (to Cleopatra)
Come now. We need not watch what will happen next.

                                   (God and Cleopatra exit, then barge
                                   back on stage. God points finger with
                                   authority.)

                              GOD
     (continuing)
Kiss the girls. I command thee!

                                   (Delbert and Simon kiss them. They
                                   roll about on the floor. God and
                                   Cleopatra applaud. All applaud, whoop
                                   it up.)

                              SIMON
Ow! Ow! She's biting me. She's a vampire!

                                   (Mary biting Simon's neck.)

                              DELBERT
Let go of me. You're hurting my ribs.

                                   (Samantha hugs tight, kissing madly.)

                                   (Simon and Delbert break away, rise up,
                                   run for exit. God snaps finger, points
                                   to door. Door locked.)

                              GOD
Be still and know I am she.

                                    (Thunder, lights flicker, everyone
                                    loses balance. Delbert and Simon
                                    scream, pound on door.)

                              DELBERT
Mom, help.

                              SIMON
Mother, take me home. I'll never step foot in a bar
again.

                                    (Gertrude, arms crossed, wags head.)

                                    (Samantha and Mary toss flowers.
                                    Wicked Pete and another man catch them,
                                    they frown. Ladies chum up to them.
                                    Stroke their hair.)

                              GOD
Come forth.

                                    (Delbert and Simon are propelled
                                    forward, they resist to no use.)

                              SIMON
     (to priest)
You're no priest, it's the Bartender!

                              DELBERT
I'll kill him. I'll wring your neck.

                                    (Priest runs behind bar. Delbert and
                                    Simon's feet stuck like in glue.)

                              MAN'S VOICE (V.O.)
Cease and desist. Stop I say.

                                    (Adam and Eve enter wearing figleafs.)

                              SIMON
It can't be.

                              DELBERT
     (to Adam)
You don't exist!

                              ADAM
I don't, huh? Feel this!

                                    (Adam punches Delbert in chest.
                                    Delbert falls down.)

                              ADAM
     (continuing)
Call me a wimp? You think you can take me? You
want a piece of me? C'mon!

(Adam's in a rage.)

GOD

Enough of this nonsense.

(Samantha helps Delbert to his feet.)

DELBERT

You! You! You tricked me!

SAMANTHA

I had to, darling. Please don't be angry with me.
I did this for you, darling. Sacrificed my
wonderful single life just to make you happy.
Believe me, honey. If I didn't cherish you I never
would have done this. See?

(Samantha bats her eyes.)

DELBERT

This is a stage play, a setup, a scam.

MARY

Was a stage play. You fell head over heals for it.
It's reality, babe. You're married!

DELBERT

It's not valid. The joke's off, folks.

SAMANTHA

(hand to heart)
It's legal. God as my witness.

EVE

That's what you think, buster. It's all on video
tape.

(Eve pushes Delbert and Samantha close
together. Delbert hesitates. God
moves hand. Delbert is pushed by the
invisible force into Samantha's face.
They kiss.)

(Mary and Simon do the same. Everyone
applauds.)

(Stagehand holds up applaud sign to
audience.)

(Delbert and Simon's hands flailing,
but they are lip-locked.)

(Adam prances around them.)

ADAM

Yeah? Well now you know what I had to go through
back in, Eden. That's right. I was forced to hook
up with, Eve. Like you, I never had a choice!

                         EVE
You bum. Dirty, filthy, lying, bum.

                         (Adam backs away as Eve.)

                         EVE
        (continuing)
It's the same ol' story I've heard for thousands of
years, and you started the ugly rumor. "I had to do
it." "I had no choice." "She made me do it."

                         ADAM
Calm down, dear. Calm, be calm.
        (to God)
God, help me!
                              (God turns her head away. Snaps
                              fingers. Delbert and Simon are free,
                              but stand gazing in Samantha's and
                              Mary's eyes.)

                         (Eve has firm grip on Adam's earlobe.)

                         EVE
Now you set the record straight, boy, cause when I
get you home there will be hell to pay.

                         (God covers her ears.)

                         GOD
Don't say that word.

                         (Devil appears, clapping his hands.)

                         GOD
        (continuing)
Go to hell.

                         DEVIL
No, please. Not there.

                              (God kicks Devil in butt. He runs into
                              ladies room.)

                         DELBERT
Simon? I'm, I'm in heaven. I feel a warmth I
thought I could never find.

                         SIMON
Delbert? My thing is hurting me--

                         DELBERT
Shut up!

                         SIMON
This thing, Delbert.

        (Simon pulls out wedding ring from his
        pocket, slips it on Mary's hand. Clock
        bell rings DONG!)

        (Mary hugs Samantha.)

       SAMANTHA
I told you it would work.

       MARY
I'm married! I'm married at last! Now I can die in
peace as Mrs... Mrs.? I don't know their last
names, do you?

        (Samantha recoils, pulls Delbert close.)

       SAMANTHA
So who am I?

       DELBERT
Mrs. Delbert Pimpleface.

        (Samantha and Mary gasp, hands over
        mouths.)

       SAMANTHA
Noooo! It can't be true! Pimpleface?

        (God shrugs shoulders.)

       CLEOPATRA
Be careful what you pray for. You'll just might get
it, babe.

       MARY
   (to Simon)
And me?

       SIMON
Mrs. Simon Crotchitch.

       MARY
Crotch-itch?

        (Samantha and Mary bust into tears.)

       MARY
   (continuing)
My tombstone will say Mrs. Crotchitch.

       SAMANTHA
Mine says, Pimpleface.

        (They bawl loudly.)

        (God rubs her temples, drinks a shot of
        Snakebite whiskey.)

                              GOD
Enough already. The deed is done. My business is
finished here.
          (to Samantha and Mary)
Don't forget, blush gently, not too much mascara,
and always use acid for the first hit.

                            PRIEST
Hit?

                              (Priest crashes through R. locked door,
                              exits, The real priest enters,
                              fighting with the Bartender/priest.)

                         REAL PRIEST
How dare you impersonate a man of honor.

                              (Gertrude jumps in, kicks, etc.)

                              (Cleopatra waves, throws a kiss to
                              audience and exits, with Wicked Pete in
                              tow.)

                              (Eve grabs Adam by the ear, leads him
                              to exit.)

                            ADAM
Ow! Ouch! Please, darling. You know I love you.
Yes, I'll take out the trash.

                           DELBERT
Trash? Trash?

                            SIMON
Uh-oh!

                             GOD
It's time for me to leave now.

                          SAMANTHA
Oh, no you don't.

                             GOD
I must leave. Many women pray for help. I created
Mademoiselle magazine for them, yet they still don't
get it.
                              (Samantha grabs God's arm, but can't
                              seem to get a grip.)

                             GOD
     (continuing)
I answered your prayers. What more do you want of
me?
                          SAMANTHA
I want to be thin! Gorgeous! Fabulously beautiful!

                             GOD
What for? You're married now.

(Samantha thinks.)

                         SAMANTHA
You're right.   What bloody for?

              SAMANTHA   MARY
          We're married now.   We're married now.

                         (Samantha and Mary approach Delbert and
                         Simon, hands outstretched to choke
                         them.)

              DELBERT   SIMON
          Uh-oh.   Uh-oh.

                         (Delbert and Simon backtrack, trip,
                         fall on couch. Samantha and Mary
                         pounce on them, twist ears.)

                         DELBERT
Ow! Honey, ow!

                         SAMANTHA
So, I'm a nasty little goonie-bird actress, huh?
And you could abuse me without my knowing, hmmm?

                         MARY
     (to Simon)
And you laughed when he said it. Didn't you?

                         SIMON
Ouch! Mary, ow!

                         (Samantha and Mary grab Delbert and
                         Simon's nose, pull them out R. exit.)

                         GOD
After all I've done for this world, and nobody
thanks me.

                         (God flicks cigarette ash on floor and
                         leaves. Thunder rumbles, lights
                         flicker. Music of Angels singing.)

                         (Devil exits from ladies room,
                         violently jabs pitchfork behind bar.)

                       A VOICE (V.O.)
Ouch! Ow! Wait for me!

                         (Cupid with heart-tipped arrows and bow
                         dashes from behind bar, Devil chases
                         Cupid out R. exit.)

     CURTAIN FALLS

AT RISE:

>   (Actors approach one-by-one and bow.
>   Samantha and Mary approach, trip and
>   fall down. Faces gawk at audience.)

>   (Delbert and Simon enter, step over
>   Samantha and Mary, bow.)

>   (Samantha and Mary's fists rise, sock
>   them on the jaw, knocking out.)

CURTAIN FALLS

(END OF SCENE F)

SCENE G

NO RISE:

>   SAMANTHA (V.O.)
> I told you, Delbert. Never to embarrass me in
> public.

>   MARY (V.O.)
> You listen to her, Simon.

>   DELBERT (V.O.)
> Ow! Ow! I'm sorry, darling. Ow!

>   SIMON (V.O.)
> Yeow! Of course I love you, Mary. Ouch!

>   SAMANTHA (V.O.)
> Tomorrow we are going to court to change our names.
> Now git home, and take out the trash.

>   DELBERT
> What of the honeymoon?

>   SAMANTHA (V.O.)   MARY (V.O.)
>   This is your honeymoon!   This is your honeymoon!

>   DELBERT (V.O.)   SIMON (V.O.)
>   Ouch! Ouch!   Ow! Ow!

>   SAMANTHA (V.O.)
> Do you understand the meaning of this?

>   END OF PLAY

CAST LIST

ACT I SCENE A

Note: Asterist (*) denotes doublecasting option. Cast list calling new characters required for scene.

Samantha Petunia Panther (age 29)
Mary Bee Canary (29)

CAST LIST (CON'T)
ACT I SCENE B

Discjockey, any age.
*Actors and Actresses 4 to 6 any age.
Delbert Pimpleface (35).
Simon Crotchitch (33).
Alex Gethigh (40).
Bartender, any age.
*1 or 2 policeman, any age.
*2 stagehands.
*3 men & 3 women, (30ish).
*2 to 3 men, *2 to 3 women (30ish).
Wicked Pete, cowboy (45).
Delores, cocktail waitress (40).
*2 women, 2 men (30ish).

CAST LIST (CON'T)
ACT II SCENE C

*6 extras, Girtrude Crotchitch, *priest, two clowns, *2 cops, God, Devil.

CAST LIST (CON'T)
ACT II SCENE D

*Cleopatra.

CAST LIST (CON'T)
ACT II SCENE E

*6 extras, *2 women (any age), *new waitress.

CAST LIST (CON'T)
ACT III SCENE F

Bartender/priest, *Adam & Eve, *stage hand, *the real priest, Cupid.

PROP LIST

ACT 1 SCENE A

Note: See diagram for fixed stage props.

2 cigarettes, 2 telephones, makeup, wine bottle, ashtray, hand mirror, panties, raccoon slippers, "Clucky Chicken" feed sack nightie, wall mirror, chocolate bars, gin bottle, 2 wall calendars.

PROP LIST (CON'T)
ACT I SCENE B

Music, red satin shirt, 2 gold chains, theatrical contract, stage play script, whiskey bottle, champagne bottle, wine bottle and 4 wine glasses, music "Newborn Friends" and "Don't Cry" by Seal (or similar), hash pipe, cigarette papers, 2 wine bottles, 2 Zinfandel wine bottles, 2 King Cobra beer cans, 2 bottles tequila, 2 makeup mirrors, small ashtray, napkins, stick deodorant, Mademoiselle magazine, can of dog food, cigarettes, bird seed cake, can of insecticide, towel, pencil, drinks on bar, drinks on a waitress tray.

PROP LIST (CON'T)
ACT II SCENE C

2 Coat & tie, 2 beers and glasses, 7 cigarettes, men's cologne, 2 whiskey bottles, 6 drink glasses, SFX device for cracking ribs, 6 wedding rings, FBI I.D. cards, Snakebite whiskey, can of insecticide, cigarettes, newspaper personal section, SFX thunder device, 2 beers.

PROP LIST (CON'T)
ACT III SCENE D

Chime bells.

PROP LIST (CON'T)
ACT III SCENE E

2 drinks, napkins, 2 pocket books, tire pressure gage, 2 diamond rings, 2 sunglasses, 2 white hats, 4 beers, quarter, paper money, 4 balloons, SFX for whistle, pair of ear rings, beer bottle, 2 handkerchiefs, pair of high heel shoes, condom in package, handcuffs, wallet, sunglasses, gold jewelry, beer bottle, pacifier nipple, paper money.

PROP LIST (CON'T)
ACT III SCENE F

2 pair cowboy boots, stage play script, rap music, 2 tuxedoes, 4 cigarettes, SFX thunder device, 2 wedding gowns, drinks on bar, 2 bouquet of flowers, applaud sign, wedding ring, SFX clock bell, Snakebite whiskey, pitchfork, bow and heart-tipped arrows.

COSTUME LIST

Critical costumes called out in script. All other clothing changes are performer's prerogative.

MUSIC CALLS

Author's call for music are demonstrative. Musical artist copyright restrictions likely apply and producer should retain permission before performing music to an audience.

THE 7 DAY PLAN TO BE A BETTER CHRISTIAN!

SUNDAY -- This is a day of rest (see Saturday) of which no work is to be performed. Take full advantage of it! However, extend extra kindness to others. Read the Word, listen to Christian radio and watch TV for faith comes by "hearing" the Word of God.

MONDAY -- Drive your vehicle with patience towards others. Be changed at work. No more gossip, complaining, bad jokes. Just start being nice -- Biblically correct! Be cooperative. Can you do this for just one day?

TUESDAY -- Forget Me! Do a good thing for another. Open doors, buy someone a meal or gift, feed a stranger's parking meter. Give so you will receive. Give something! The Lord gives, so should you.

WEDNESDAY -- Compliment Day! Say something nice to someone, including one who may not like you. Be sincere about it! If someone needs help, go to their aid. Make someone smile today!

THURSDAY -- Distribute a Bible track. No tracks? Make or buy some! It is time you begin your ministry to the Lord to share the Good News. There are many hurting people who need the Lord and it is your responsibility to introduce them to Him. Using tracks make the job easy!

FRIDAY -- Day of forgiveness! When you forgive others transgressions, you are released from the anguish within yourself. It is easy to do! Start the process today! See Tuesday and Wednesday's instructions. Life is so much easier to live and great mercy and blessing arrive when you forgive!

SATURDAY -- Rest if this is the Sabbath you honor or donate; time, items, food, or money to the homeless shelters. Do not forget the poor! Visit or call a relative or friend. Express your appreciation for what the Lord has given you! Share with others what you have and the Lord will give you even more!

James Russell Publishing 780 Diogenes Drive, Reno, NV 89512

Free Bible Tracks For SASE!

EACH DAY

Contact Us For Bible Tracks!

START the day right by greeting the Lord and giving thanks for all He has done and what He will do for you in the future. **END** the day right by expressing your gratitude to the Lord.

SPEAK often to the Lord, as he is your best friend. Remember, he wants to handle every detail in your life, even the small stuff. Do not become so busy in your day you leave Him out of your life.

WHEN you pray just speak as you would to a friend. There is no need for theatrical displays of emotions or insincerity. If you fall short, do not turn your face away from the Lord and hide. Take the issue to Him.

WHAT will you give to the Lord if He grants your request? Will you simply say thank you and forget Him until you need something else later? The Lord sees the suffering of the sick and poor. Why not pledge to help them? Make your promise and keep it! Do it now before you recieve. This is faith in action.

SPREAD the Word of God. You may not be a minister, but you can distribute tracks. Leave them everywhereyou go. Keep some on your person each day. Your reward shall be great! Write us for tracts!

TITHE to the Lord. Give and you shall recieve more! Give to churches, ministries, homeless shelters, or where there is dire need. A perfect expression of love for others! God's System Never Fails!

PRINT AND DISTRIBUTE TO OTHERS!

JAMES RUSSELL PUBLISHING

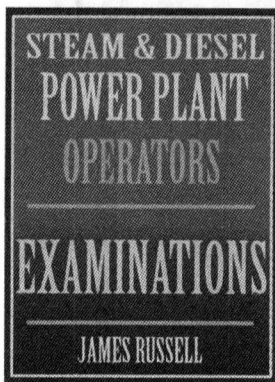

www.ingramcontent.com/pod-product-compliance
Lightning Source LLC
Chambersburg PA
CBHW081152090426

42736CB00017B/3293